The Short
of Robert H

In the Older Scottish Ton

Published by DoubleBridge Press,
The Publications Group of
Dunfermline Heritage Community Projects

ISBN 978-0-9557244-6-6

Management and Production by Clive Willcocks,
DHCP Publications Group Leader
Design and typesetting by Oliver Boyd, Graphic Designer
Illustrations by Alan Batley

The sign of the DoubleBridge Press is derived from the celebrated Double Bridge in Pittencrieff Glen, Dunfermline, Fife, Scotland.

Foreword

I am delighted to see this decades-long labour of love finally brought to the press, and equally delighted to have been asked to provide the Foreword to what I hope will be only the first of a series of publications of Robert Henryson's poetry designed to make his work more accessible to the more general reader, particularly in his home county of Fife.

The Robert Henryson Society, based in Dunfermline, was founded by the late Dr. George Philp in 1993, with the hope that 'the auld grey toun' as George always referred to Dunfermline, would take the poet to its heart. Part of the Society's mission was to bring the poet's work to teachers in the local schools, and in this Barbara Rasmusen was instrumental. As an advisor in Primary Education, she had access to all the schools and teachers, and began producing her translations of Henryson's Fables in a form designed to appeal to younger children, and to give teachers an aid in their introduction of these poems to their pupils. This very practical beginning was the springboard of her work in translating the complete works over a period of years.

I have worked with Barbara for longer than I care to remember, suggesting refinements to the translations on occasion, but in the main celebrating and supporting the excellent work she has produced, which is based on sound scholarship and detailed reading of the texts and secondary critical material. There will be those who say that Henryson should not be translated as the Middle Scots language is not very difficult to understand, but perhaps this is the reason that Henryson is so little known and appreciated outside academia. As the late great Seamus Healy found a deep connection in the works of Henryson which inspired him to make his regrettably few translations, Barbara shows throughout this work her passion for Henryson's thoughts, ideas and language.

We are indebted to Dunfermline Heritage Community Projects for having the confidence to publish this volume as a taster for a longer series.

Morna R. Fleming, Secretary, The Robert Henryson Society, May 2016

Acknowledgements

I wish to thank all those who have supported me in various ways throughout my work on the translation of Robert Henryson's poetry. In particular I would like to thank Morna Fleming, Secretary of The Robert Henryson Society for her help and input during the early years and for her on-going support during the process of the translation. Without her, there would have been no publication. I also give thanks to all those who have read and expressed their opinions concerning the translations, namely my husband David Rasmusen, my sisters, Isabella Robertson, Elizabeth Muir and Margaret Stewart and my nephew, John Stewart. There are many others who have also given their reactions and comments about the translated poetry. I thank them also. I am indebted to Clive Willcocks and the Committee of Dunfermline Heritage Community Projects, for undertaking the production of this volume which I hope will lead to a greater interest in Robert Henryson's poetry and in early Scottish literature.

Barbara Rasmusen

Contents

Introduction

The Aims of the Translation

Robert Henryson, one of the Scottish makars, a group of medieval poets, was the most important poet of 15th century Scotland. This translation of his poetry is aimed at promoting access to his works and to the literary heritage of the Scottish people.

It is not the intention that the translation should detract from the original poems or from the quality of Henryson's work and every attempt has been made to retain the original meaning, style, metre, and rhyme. In some cases the metre and rhyme have been sacrificed so that the meaning can be retained.

The original and translated texts have been placed side by side for ease of reference. Initial reading of the translation may be followed by an interlinked study of the two texts, leading to greater appreciation of the original poetry and to a more in-depth knowledge of the Older Scottish Tongue. In this way a wider audience will be able to read not only the poetry of Henryson but also the works of other medieval Scottish writers.

Background Information: Robert Henryson

Details of Henryson's life are limited but the name Robert Henryson is said to have appeared in several historical documents and records. In the records of the University of Glasgow on September 10, 1462 'the Venerable Master Robert Henryson, Licentiate in Arts and Bachelor in Decrees, was incorporated' i.e. admitted as a member of the university. A man called Robert Henryson also taught in St Andrews for a short period. No one knows if either of these men was Robert Henryson, the poet.

However Master Robert Henryson, the writer of *The Moral Fables* and other poems is thought to have been for a time a notary and school master in Dunfermline, Fife. His name appears as a witness on charters from the Benedictine abbey in Dunfermline so a connection with either of the men identified in the previous paragraph is possible.

Men of such standing usually had attended a university either in Scotland or in Europe before they could be called 'Master'. If Henryson were a graduate from a university, in his youth he would have lived the kind of life students lived at that time. Their life was not easy, the students working long and hard. The following is a description of the routine of Paris University, which would have been similar to that of other medieval universities if they chose to follow it. (Source – Quatercentenary of the death of Hector Boece, 1936)

A bell was struck at four in the morning and lectures began at five o'clock. Mass was said at six o'clock followed by a breakfast of half a loaf of bread or a small white loaf. After the ringing of the bell at eight o'clock, studying began and continued until ten o'clock. Formal debates followed for an hour. Divine Service was held at noon followed by an hour-long meal when excerpts from the Bible and the lives of saints were read. After the meal artists and grammarians would be listened to. From the third to the fifth hour lectures were given and disputations were held from the fifth to the sixth hour. After the evening meal work would continue until nine o'clock when a signal to retire for the night would be given. This signal was often delayed until ten o'clock. No student was allowed to study after ten o'clock. A student's day, if this was the routine followed, could be anything from seventeen to nineteen hours long including meal times. Local variations would, of course, occur.

Henryson is identified as 'School Master of Dunfermline' on the title page of his fables printed in 1570 and 1571 and again on the print of Cresseid in 1593, probably the result of this designation appearing on older copies of Henryson's poetry. Schooling took place in church schools where the boys were taught reading, writing and the singing of church music.

Towards the end of the century grammar/burgh schools came into being. The term 'grammar' arose from the fact that, as the teaching of Latin was so important, Latin grammar held a prominent position in the teaching in the schools. It is believed that Henryson both taught in and supervised the running of the grammar school for the burgh of Dunfermline.

An Act of Parliament had been passed in 1496 and contained the following:

> It is statute and ordained through all the realm that all barons and freeholders put their eldest sons and heirs to the school from that they be eight or nine years of age and to remain at the grammar schools till they be competently established and have perfect Latin and thereafter to remain three years at the schools of art and law so that they may have knowledge and understanding of the laws through the which justice may reign universally through all the realm so that they that are sheriffs or judges under the king's highness may have knowledge to do justice so that the poor people should have no need to seek our sovereign lord's principal auditors for each small injury.

Any baron or freeholder who did not send his son to school had to pay the sum of twenty Scots pounds to the king.

From a reading of Henryson's poems it is possible to discover some information about his personality, beliefs and knowledge.

- He displays a wry sense of humour, an ability to portray characters in a humane and compassionate manner, and to convey his own ideas and beliefs. He claims to write in 'hamelie language and termis rude' but the actuality is that he displays a strong command of the language he uses. He writes in a manner and style familiar to his listeners and readers, varying both to suit his chosen audience in order to connect with them clearly.

- He wrote the poems with a serious purpose i.e. to give a strong moral message to all and advice to sinners including members of the church and the nobility. The poems were adapted to reflect the tenets, ideas, behaviour and culture of the country in which he lived.

- He had an in-depth knowledge of the courts of law and the procedures for trials. He believed that some of the courts were conducted in an illegal manner and that poor or innocent people were at the mercy of unjust men. The law courts were very busy during the latter part of the century due to deep-seated economic difficulties, which plagued medieval society at this time. Quarrels over wills, debts, rents, breaches of contracts, land tenure etc. were rife and led to litigation.

- He was an educated man with an in-depth knowledge of the bible and other works studied at universities at that time.

- He had the commonly held knowledge of the time of both astrology and astronomy, which were used conjointly in medieval times, and of the gods and goddesses and their relationships to the planets.

- He believed that the plague was sent by God to punish men for all the wicked activities that were occurring.

- He saw God as a wrathful god.

The Short Poems

This book contains the short poems of Henryson in the Older Scottish Tongue and in translation, with accompanying notes. The volume does not seek to become an academic work. It seeks to reveal some of Henryson's original purpose, i.e. to arouse interest, to entertain, to educate, to make readers aware of a strong moral code and appropriate behavior, as well as giving the readers some insight to language of The Older Scottish Tongue.

The poems are miscellaneous in subject, referring to spiritual and behavioural matters, some presented in a satirical manner.

Poetry Theme	Intended 15th Century Audience and Aims
Robene and Makyne A pastoral – telling the tale of a country couple, following the precepts of courtly love, inappropriately.	To make a jibe at courtly love practice as it was undertaken by country people. To include a subtext regarding chastity. To make men aware of the falsity of women.
The Bludy Serk The tale of a knight rescuing a fair maiden from the clutches of an ugly giant at the behest of her father, the knight dying as a result of the wounds received in the fight.	To illustrate to those of the Christian faith, through the various characterisations, the sacrifice made by Jesus Christ in His role as the saviour of their souls.

Poetry Theme	Intended 15th Century Audience and Aims
The Garmont of Gude Ladeis Allegorical inventory of the garments of women used to list the behavioural attributes most required in 'gude ladeis'.	To draw women's attention to Timothy Book 1, Chapter 2. which contains an admonishment to women regarding their dress, their behavioural attributes, and their relationship with men. Piety is advocated.
The Prais of Aige In this poem an old man decries the state of the world as he finds it. He is embittered and looks to death for relief.	To point out to readers, young and old, the problems that face Youth in the troubled society. He puts forward for consideration the problems of the ageing process and the loss of enjoyment in life that age brings so that death is welcomed.
The Ressoning betwixt Aige and Youth A young man and an old man meet. The older man carries a banner warning of the fleeting nature of life. The young man challenges the statement.	To make younger men aware of the transitory nature of life and the weaknesses of the flesh which occur as one grows older. Age warns them that their present physical state will soon disappear leaving them in the condition in which he now finds himself.
The Abbay Walk During a walk near the abbey the poet sees graffiti written on a wall, giving advice to Christians.	To pass on the advice to his readers that, no matter what befalls you, you accept it and cope with it, not blaming God for your misfortunes.
The Ressoning betwix Deth and Man. The persona of Death approaches Man warning him that death comes to all. Man, at first, challenges him but then reveals he has sinned and will be found wanting upon his death.	To make younger men aware that death cannot be escaped through status, wealth, bodily strength or youth, and must be prepared for by repentance and prayer.
Aganis Haisty Credence of Titlaris A poem concerning the behaviour of those who report falsely to those in authority in order to influence the results.	To point out to those in authority, lords, judges, churchmen, that in making judgements, one source of information should not be taken at its face value but should be corroborated by statements from more than one witness.

Poetry Theme	Intended 15th Century Audience and Aims
The Annunciation A retelling of the angel Gabriel's visit to Mary with God's message of the Incarnation.	To emphasise the purity of Mary, Mother of God. To retell the details of Gabriel's visit and to acknowledge previous interventions made by God on earth.
Sum Practysis of Medecyne A damning, satirical look at the medical profession through the description of some dubious prescriptions.	To indicate to the readers his utter disillusionment with the practices of apothecaries. To make the apothecaries take note of his feelings and his complete lack of regard for their cures.
The Thre Dead Pollis In this poem the three death's heads point out the frailty of life, the necessity for repentance, and the need for prayers for the souls of the dead.	To remind the readers that all mankind will meet the fate of the heads no matter their station in life, how they looked or what their occupation was. To repent is essential as are prayers for the absolving of the souls of the dead. To make judgements about character based on looks is unwise.
Ane Prayer for the Pest This poem addresses Jesus directly by means of a prayer admitting that Man has broken God's law and has been punished by God by the coming of the plague. The penitent seeks God's forgiveness and the removal of the plague.	To tell all his readers that the plague had been caused by Man's fall from grace in the sight of the Lord. To inform those in charge of meting out justice that it was their duty to enforce the law and punish sinners. To beg Jesus to be merciful to those whom He saved by the spilling of His blood.
The Want of Wyse Men The poem states that the lack of educated men amongst those with authority has caused poor government, instability, injustice, poverty and unlawfulness, resulting in upheaval in the land.	To make those ruling the land aware that the situation caused by the appointment of unsuitable, badly educated men is to the detriment of the kingdom. To ask those in authority to recognise that education is essential for the successful governing of the kingdom.

Robene and Makyne

Robene and Makyne

Robene sat on gud grene hill,
Kepand a flok of fe:
Mirry Makyne said him till,
'Robene, thow rew on me;
I haif the luvit lowd and still,
Thir yeiris two or three;
My dule in dern, bot gif thow dill,
Dowtles but dreid I de.'

Robene answerit, 'Be the rude,
Nathing of lufe I knaw,   10
Bot keipis my scheip undir yone wude,
Lo, quhair thay raik on raw;
Quhat hes marrit the in thy mude,
Makyne, to me thow schaw;
Or quhat is lufe? or to be lude?
Fane wald I leir that law.'

'At luvis lair gife thow will leir,
Tak thair ane A, B, C:
Be heynd, courtass, and fair of feir,
Wyse, hardy and fre;   20
So that no denger do the deir,
Quhat dule in dern thow dre;
Preiss the with pane at all poweir,
Be patient and previe.'

Robene answerit hir agane,
'I wait nocht quhat is luve;
Bot I haif mervell in certane
Quhat makis the this wanrufe:
The weddir is fair, and I am fane,
My scheip gois hail aboif;   30
And we wald play us in this plane,
Thay wald us bayth reproif.'

'Robene, tak tent unto my taill,
And wirk all as I reid,
And thow sall haif my hairt all haill,
Eik and my madinheid.
Sen God sendis bute for baill,
And for murnyng remeid,
I dern with the, bot gif I daill,
Doutles I am bot deid.'   40

12

Robene and Makyne

Robene sat on a fine green hill,
Where he his sheep could see.
Merry Makyne said with a will,
'Robene please pity me.
I have loved you openly and still
These years two or three.
My secret anguish makes me ill,
Doubtless the death of me.'

Robene answered, 'By the rood (cross),
Nothing of love I know,   10
But keep my sheep in this wood,
Lo, where they feed in a row.
What has marred you in the mood
Makyne, that to me you show?
What is love, or to be loved?
Surely I would like to know.'

'At love's school if you seek learning,
Take then an A, B, C.
Be gentle, courteous, fair of bearing,
Wise, generous and free,   20
So that no danger you are dreading,
Or have a secret trouble thee.
Contend with pain with strong bearing.
Be patient, all in privacy.'

Robene answered her again,
'I know not what love is,
But that I have wondered is certain
What puts you in such distress.
I am happy and there is no rain,
My sheep, safe and harmless ,   30
And if we lie close on this plain
Us they would censor doubtless.'

'Robene pay attention to my tale,
And do as I have said,
And you shall have my heart so leal (loyal),
And also my maidenhead.
Since God sends us help for such torments
And solace for our cries and our laments.
In secret with you unless I deal,
Doubtless I am but dead.'   40

'Makyne, to morne this ilk a tyde,
And ye will meit me heir,
Peraventure my scheip ma gang besyd,
Quhill we haif liggit full neir;
Bot maugre haif I and I byd,
Fra thay begin to steir;
Quhat lyis on hairt I will nocht hyd;
Makyne, than mak gud cheir.'

'Robene, thow reivis me roif and rest;
I luve bot the allone.'   50
'Makyne, adew, the sone gois west,
The day is neirhand gone.'
'Robene, in dule I am so drest,
That lufe wil be my bone.'
'Ga lufe, Makyne, quhairevir thow list,
For lemman I lue none.'

'Robene I stand in sic a styll;
I sich, and that full sair.'
'Makyne, I haif bene heir this quhyle;
At hame God gif I wair.'   60
'My huny, Robene, talk ane quhyll,
Gif thow will do na mair.'
'Makyne, sum uthir man begyle,
For hamewart I will fair.'

Robene on his wayis went,
Als licht as leif of tre;
Mawkin murnit in hir intent,
And trowd him nevir to se.
Robene brayd attour the bent;
Than Mawkyne cryit on hie,   70
'Now ma thow sing, for I am schent!
Quhat alis lufe at me?'

Mawkyne went hame withowttin faill,
Full wery eftir cowth weip:
Than Robene in a ful fair daill
Assemblit all his scheip.
Be that sum pairte of Mawkynis aill
Outthrow his hairt cowd creip;
He fallowit hir fast thair till assaill,
And till hir tuke gude keip.   80

'Abyd! abyd! thow fair Makyne,
A word for ony thing;
For all my luve it sal be thyne,
Withowttin depairting.
All haill, thy harte for till haif myne

14

'Makyne, tomorrow at this tide,
If you will meet me here,
Peradventure my sheep may stay beside
While we have lain full near.
Blamed I shall be if by your side
I stay and they move off from here.
What lies in my heart I will not hide;
Makyne, then make good cheer.'

'Robene, you rob me of peace and rest.
I love but you alone.'   50
'Makyne, adieu, the sun goes west.
The day is near hand gone.'
'Robene, so deep in sorrow I am pressed
That my life by love will be done.'
'Go love, Makyne, where ever you list
For sweetheart I love none.'

'Robene, I stand in such a style.
I sigh full sore, as you see.'
'Makyne, I have been here this while.
God grant, at home I wish to be.'   60
'My honey, Robene, talk a while
If you will do no more.'
'Makyne, some other man beguile,
For homeward I will flee.'

Robene on his way then went,
As light as a leaf on a tree.
Makyne mourned, her mind intent,
And vowed him never to see.
Robene cried out as he went,
And Makyne cried on high,   70
'Now may you sing, for I am spent.
What ails love at me?'

Makyne went home without fail,
Full weary, after did weep.
Then Robene in a lovely dale
Assembled all his sheep.
When some part of Makyne's tale,
Throughout his heart did creep.
He followed her quickly there to assail,
And good heed to her did keep.   80

'Stay! Stay! you fair Makyne,
A word for anything;
For all my love it shall be thine,
Without once departing.
Truly, your heart to have as mine

Is all my cuvating;
My scheip to morne quhill houris nyne
Will neid of no keping.'

'Robene, thow hes hard soung and say,
In gestis and storeis auld,   90
"The man that will nocht quhen he may
Sall haif nocht quhen he wald."
I pray to Jesu every day
Mot eik thair cairis cauld,
That first preisis with the to play,
Be firth, forrest, or fawld.'

'Makyne, the nicht is soft and dry,
The wedder is warm and fair,
And the grene woid rycht neir us by
To walk attour all-quhair;   100
Thair ma na janglour us espy,
That is to lufe contrair;
Thairin, Makyne, bath ye and I
Unsene we ma repair.'

'Robene, that warld is all away
And quyt brocht till ane end,
And nevir agane thairto perfay
Sall it be as thow wend;
For of my pane thow maid it play,
And all in vane I spend;   110
As thow hes done, sa sall I say,
Murne on, I think to mend.'

'Mawkyne, the howp of all my heill,
My hairt on the is sett,
And evirmair to the be leill,
Quhill I may leif but lett;
Nevir to faill, as utheris feill,
Quhat grace that evir I gett.'
'Robene, with the I will nocht deill;
Adew, for thus we mett.'   120

Malkyne went hame blyth anneuche,
Attour the holtis hair;
Robene murnit, and Makyne leuche;
Scho sang; he sichit sair;
And so left him, baith wo and wreuche,
In dolour and in cair,
Kepand his hird under a huche,
Amangis the holtis hair.

Is all I am wanting.
My sheep tomorrow till hour nine,
Will have no need of keeping.'

'Robene, you have heard what they say
In tales and stories old.   90
"The man who will not when he may,
Shall not have when feeling bold."
I pray to Jesus every day
To make their loving cold,
That first seeks with you to play,
By firth, forest or fold.'

'Makyne, the night is soft and dry.
The weather is warm and fair,
And the greenwood right near us by
To walk about everywhere;   100
There may no gossip us espy
That is to love contrair.
Therein, Makyne, both you and I
Unseen may we repair.'

'Robene that world is all away,
And to an end quite brought,
And never again in this present way
Shall it be as you once thought.
For of my pain you made a play,
And all in vain I was fraught.   110
As you have done so shall I say,
Mourn on. I will recover as I ought.'

'Makyne, the hope of my salvation,
My heart on you is set,
And ever more to you is loyal
As long as I live yet.
Never to fail as others fail,
What grace that ever I get.'
'Robene with thee I will not deal.
Adieu, for thus we met,'   120

Makyne went home satisfied,
Through the woods hoar grey.
Robene mourned, and Makyne laughed.
She sang, he sighed sorely.
And so left him, mournful and sad,
In pain in every way
Under a hillside, keeping his herd,
Amongst the woods that day.

'Robene and Makyne' is one of the earliest, if not the earliest, pastoral in Scottish poetry. Pastoral poetry depicts examples of rural life in particular that of shepherds, usually in an idealistic manner.

The characters in such poetry are often used to illustrate the moral and social views held by the writer. Henryson, in this poem, appears to challenging the dictates of Courtly Love by producing a skit on such love but a secondary purpose may also be contained in the poem. The church, at the time, suggested, with reference to the writings of Thomas Aquinas, that a degree of celibacy, temporary abstinence, would provide the opportunity to increase personal spirituality. Men were urged to control their natural desires even in the case of their wives. Women were often portrayed as temptresses. Marriages of nobles were usually arranged marriages where acquisition of goods, status and power were the reasons for them taking place. Love was not part of the equation. It had to be sought outside the marriage but any relationship was expected to be platonic in nature.

Line 5	lowd and still – openly and secretly – continually but in secret where necessary (a figure from the romances).
Lines 17- 24	Courtly love (12th-14th century) was a code of behaviour the rules of which were drawn up in the late 12th century by Andreas Capellanus. Many scholars say that it was intended to be a 'pure love', one which ennobled, which led to adoration of the beloved and which was never satisfied, leading to increasing desire. The reality may have been somewhat different. The long list of rules prescribed the behaviour between a knight and a revered, usually married, lady and progressed through a number of stages in a long-term secret relationship.

1. Initial attraction, conveyed by glances and looks.

2. No direct approach is made, the knight worshipping the lady from afar.

3. The knight reveals the nature of his feelings to the lady, declaring his passion.

4. The lady, keeping within the bounds of loyalty and chastity, rejects his approach.

5. The knight continues to approach the lady, declaring his honorable intentions, devotion, and suitability.

6. The knight demonstrates that he is suffering physically and emotionally because of his love for the lady. He is, in fact, lovesick.

7. The knight seeks to prove his worth and his love by undertaking difficult and dangerous tasks.

8. Physical contact is made, sometimes resulting in consummation of the love.

9. An on-going affair is conducted in all possible secrecy.

Henryson has taken the subject of Courtly Love and placed it in a rural setting, the knight becomes a shepherd and the lady a country maiden. The name Robene is the name often used for a country man while Makyne was sometimes the name given to a woman of ill-repute. Henryson changes the roles of the characters, Robene being the wooed and Maykne the wooer.

Stages of their love within their long term relationship.

Lines 1-9.	The initial relationship between the two has been in place for two to three years. Maykne now reveals the depth and nature of her true feelings.
Lines 10-18	Robene denies all knowledge of love, content with his situation in looking after his sheep. He questions Maykne's attitude, asking what is wrong.
Lines 19-24	Maykne lists the attributes required in a partner. He must be gentle, well mannered, good-looking, wise, generous and free. He must have no great fears or problems and be able to bear pain. Overall he must be patient and able to keep secrets. All these apply in the behavior defined in Courtly Love.
Lines 25-32	Robene again denies all knowledge of what love is but recognises that Maykne is in a distressed state.
Lines 33-40	Maykne states her wish to consummate their relationship and details the depth of her suffering – lovesickness unto death.
Lines 41-48	Robene says they should meet again next day but his concern for his sheep appears to be uppermost in his mind.
Lines 49-56	Maykne again professes her love but Robene rejects her again saying he has no sweetheart.
Lines 57-64	Maykne pleads with Robene to at least talk but he tells her to find another man to beguile.
Lines 65-72	The two part, one in good spirits, the other distraught.
Lines 73-80	Robene has time to think and changes his mind.
Lines 81-88	Maykne's wooing appears to have taken effect.
Lines 89-96	Maykne now rejects Robene. His now positive response has come too late.
Lines 97-104	Robene tries now to woo Maykne.
Lines 105-112	Maykne claims she has suffered too much for the sake of love and he has made light of her protestations of it.
Lines 113-120	Robene swears allegiance to her but Maykne rejects his advances and bids him 'adieu'.
Lines 121-128	The wooing has reached its conclusion with Maykne laughing and singing as she leaves him to his sheep and his sighs.

Maykne, in her male role, is portrayed as the aggressive one of a pair of lovers. In spite of the rules for Courtly Love, women were often portrayed as being corrupt, faithless and false and this can be discerned in Maykne's action of apparently more than encouraging Robene and then later refusing to react to his advances, laughing at him as she leaves.

The Bludy Serk

The Bludy Serk

This hindir yeir I hard be tald
Thair was a worthy king;
Dukis, erlis, and barronis bald
He had at his bidding.
The lord was anceance and ald,
And sexty yeiris cowth ring;
He had a dochter fair to fald,
A lusty lady ying.

Of all fairheid scho bur the flour,
And eik hir faderis air,   10
Of lusty laitis and he honour,
Meik bot and debonair.
Scho wynnit in a bigly bour;
On fold wes none so fair;
Princis luvit hir paramour,
In cuntreis our allquhair.

Thair dwelt alyt besyde the king
A fowll gyane of ane;
Stollin he hes the lady ying,
Away with hir is gane,   20
And kest hir in his dungering,
Quhair licht scho micht se nane;
Hungir and cauld and grit thristing
Scho fand in to hir wame.

He wes the laithliest on to luk
That on the grund mycht gang;
His nailis wes lyk ane hellis cruk,
Thairwith fyve quarteris lang.
Thair wes nane that he ourtuk,
In rycht or yit in wrang,   30
Bot all in schondir he thame schuke –
The gyane wes so strang.

He held the lady day and nycht
Within his deip dungeoun;
He wald nocht gif of hir a sicht,
For gold nor yit ransoun;
Bot gife the king mycht get a knycht,
To fecht with his persoun,
To fecht with him both day and nycht,
Quhill ane wer dungin doun.   40

The Bloody Shirt

This other year I heard it told
There was a worthy king;
Dukes, earls, and barons bold
He had at his bidding.
The lord was ancient and old,
Some sixty years reigning;
He had a daughter fair to hold,
A maiden, so beguiling.

Of all beauty she was the flower,
And also her father's heir,   10
Of good manners and great honour.
Meek but also debonair,
She lived in a pleasant bower;
On earth was none so fair;
Princes loved her with desire,
In countries, everywhere.

There dwelt, nearby the king,
A giant, a very foul one;
Stolen he has the lady young,
And away with her has gone,   20
Her in his dungeon casting,
Where light she might see none.
Hunger, cold and great thirsting
Into her innards did come.

He was the most loathsome on to look
That did on the earth belong;
His nails were like a devil's crook,
Therewith five quarters long.
There was none that he overtook,
In right or yet in wrong,   30
But all asunder he them shook –
The giant was so strong.

He held the lady, day and night
Within his deep dungeon;
He would not give of her a sight,
For gold or yet ransom:
Unless the king might get a knight
To fight with him in person –
To fight with him both day and night,
Till one was knocked right down.   40

The king gart seik baith fer and neir,
Beth be se and land,
Of ony knycht gife he micht heir
Wald fecht with that gyand.
A worthy prince that had no peir
Hes tane the deid on hand,
For the luve of the lady cleir,
And held full trew cunnand.

That prince come prowdly to the toun
Of that gyane to heir,   50
And fawcht with him his awin persoun,
And tuke him presoneir;
And kest him in his awin dungeoun,
Allane, withouttin feir,
With hungir, cauld, and confusioun,
As full weill worthy weir.

Syne brak the bour, had hame the bricht,
Unto hir fader deir;
Sa evill wondit was the knycht
That he behuvit to de.   60
Unlusum was his likame dicht,
His sark was all bludy;
In all the warld was thair a wicht
So peteouss for to se?

The lady murnyt and maid grit mone,
With all hir mekle micht:
'I luvit nevir lufe bot one,
That dulfully now is dicht.
God sen my lyfe were fra me tone,
Or I had sene yone sicht,   70
Or ellis in begging evir to gone
Furth with yone curtase knycht.'

He said, 'Fair Lady, now mone I
De, trestly ye me trow;
Tak ye my sark that is bludy,
And hing it forrow yow;
First think on it, and syne on me,
Quhen men cumis yow to wow.'
The Lady said, 'Be Mary free
Thairto I mak a vow.'   80

24

The king bade seek both far and near,
Both by sea and land,
For any knight if he might hear
Who against that giant would stand.
A worthy prince that had no peer
Has taken the deed on hand,
For the love of the lady dear,
And held faithfully to the plan.

That prince came proudly to the town,
Of that giant to hear,   50
And fought with him, his own person,
And took him prisoner;
And cast him in his own dungeon,
Alone, without a fellow other
With hunger, cold, and confusion,
As it full worthy were.

Then broke the bower, took home the lady,
Unto her father nigh;
So badly wounded was the knight
That he behove to die.   60
His body-blow an awful sight.
His shirt all bloody;
In all the world was there a wight
So piteous then to see?

The lady lamented and made great moan,
With all of her great might:
'I loved never love but one;
Dolefully hurt in the fight.
God grant my life had from me gone
Before I had seen that sight,   70
Or else in begging ever to have gone
Forth with that courteous knight.'

He said, 'Fair lady, now must I die,
You must believe me true;
Take you my shirt that is bloody,
And hang it in front of you;
First think on it, and then on me,
When men come you to woo.'
The lady said, 'By Gracious Mary
Thereto I promise you.'   80

Quhen that scho lukit to the serk,
Scho thocht on the persoun,
And prayit for him with all hir harte,
That lowsd hir of bandoun,
Quhair scho was wont to sit full merk
In that deip dungeoun;
And evir quhill scho wes in quert,
That was hir a lessoun.

Sa weill the lady luvit the knycht,
That no man wald scho tak.   90
Sa suld we do our God of micht,
That did all for us mak;
Quhilk fullely to deid wes dicht
For sinfull manis saik;
Sa suld we do both day and nycht,
With prayaris to Him mak.

MORALITAS.

This king is lyk the Trinitie,
Baith in hevin and heir;
The manis saule to the lady;
The gyane to Lucefeir;   100
The knycht to Chryst, that deit on tre,
And coft our synnis deir;
The pit to hell with panis fell;
The syn to the woweir.

The lady was wowd, bot scho said, 'Nay,'
With men that wald hir wed;
Sa suld we wryth all syn away,
That in our breist is bred.
I pray to Jesu Chryst verrey,
For us His blud that bled,   110
To be our help on domysday,
Quhair lawis are straitly led.

The saule is Godis dochtir deir,
And eik His handewerk,
That was betrasit with Lucifeir,
Quha sittis in hell full merk.
Borrowit with Chrystis angell cleir,
Hend men, will ye nocht herk?
For His lufe that bocht us deir,
Think on the bludy serk.   120

When she looked at the shirt,
She thought on the person,
And prayed for him, with all her heart,
Who had freed her from subjection,
When she had sat in darkest dark,
Alone in that deep dungeon;
Now every time she sat well, alert,
She was reminded of his lesson.

So well the lady loved the knight,
That no man would she take.   90
So should we do for our God of might,
That did all for us make,
Who fully to death was done,
For sinful man's sake.
So should we do both day and night,
With prayers to Him to make.

MORAL

This king is like the Trinity,
Both in heaven and here;
The man's soul to the lady;
The giant to Lucifer;   100
The knight to Christ that died on the tree
And paid for our sins dear;
The pit to hell, with pains fell,
The sin, to the wooer.

`The lady was wooed, but she said, 'Nay,'
To men that would her wed.
So should we drive all sin away
That in our breast is bred.
I pray to Jesus Christ always,
For us His blood that bled,   110
To be our help on Doomsday,
Where laws are strictly led.

The soul is God's daughter dear,
And also his handiwork,
That was betrayed by Lucifer,
Who sits in hell most dark,
Redeemed by Christ, angel, clear,
Gentle men will you not hark?
For His love that bought us dear,
Think on 'The Bludy Serk'.   120

Notes

The Title – The Bludy Serk – The bloody shirt.
The shirt worn by knights between the padded under garment and the suit of armour had the
coat of arms of the knight placed on it to identify the body if he died in battle. Sometimes a shirt,
called a surcoat, was worn on top of the armour instead with the same purpose in mind.
Lines from 'Sir Gawain and the Castle of Carlisle' illustrate the point:

> 'Ther hynge mony a blody serk
> And eche of hime a dyvers mark.'
> (Lines 535- 536)
> There hung many a bloody shirt
> And on each of them a coat of arms.

Line 28   'Thairwith five quarteris lang'. Five quarters of an ell – about 46 inches

Line 100   Lucifer,the light-bringer, was originally, in classical times, the name given to the
planet Venus when it appeared above the eastern horizon before sunrise. In the
Bible it is the name given to one of God's archangels. He was cast out of heaven
for challenging God's authority by leading a revolt of the angels.

'I saw Satan fall like lightning from heaven.' (Luke Chapter 10, verse 18) was
interpreted as the fall of Lucifer and the name Lucifer was regarded as the name
for Satan before his fall from heaven.

Background Information
The story originated in Gesta Romanorum, a Latin collection of anecdotes and tales used by
preachers which was written in the 13th to 14th centuries.
'The Emperor's Daughter' which bears more resemblance to Henryson's poem appears in a later
version and is retold here:

The Emperor's Daughter.
There once lived an emperor who had a daughter of unimaginable beauty. He loved her so dearly
that he commanded five of his trusted and brave knights to watch over her, day and night, and
if they failed their lives would be forfeited. As instructed they guarded her room, where a lamp
burned above the door so that anyone who approached could be seen easily. A large dog sat on
the threshold barking loudly when people came at all near. As you will read these precautions
were to no avail. The princess loved all the excitements of life and wanted to go out into the
world. One day as she stood looking from her window a certain duke rode by. When he saw
the princess he wanted to possess her and her father's throne. Day after day he tried all the
ways he could to get the princess to leave her room. At last by promising her untold delights he
persuaded her to overturn the burning lamp and to give the dog poisoned meat. Late at night,
with the light quenched and the dog dead, the duke stole away with the princess. The next day
the emperor's men set out to find the fugitives. One of knights, the fiercest and strongest, found
their tracks and fought and killed the duke. He returned the princess to her father who showed
his anger by placing her in solitude. Eventually all was resolved and the princess was betrothed to
a nobleman of wealth and power.

Moral
The emperor is God and his daughter is the human soul, which he protects by the five senses.
The burning lamp is the will, shining brightly in good works and dispelling the gloom of sin. The

guard dog is conscience watching out on the world and its dangers, watching for the breaking of any of the Lord's commandments. Then comes the devil extinguishing the lamp of the soul and silencing the barking of the conscience. God is our saviour fighting for our souls against the world, the flesh, the devil, taking back the soul to the palace of the heavenly king.

Henryson's Version.
Moral.
The king is the Trinity, Father, Son and Holy Ghost. The lady is Man's soul captured by the devil (the giant) and set free by Jesus (the knight).

The Garmont of Gud Ladeis

The Garmont of Gud Ladeis

Wald my gud lady lufe me best,
And wirk eftir my will,
I suld ane garmond gudliest
Gar mak hir body till.

Of he honour suld be hir hud,
Upon hir heid to weir,
Garneist with governance so gud,
Na demyng suld hir deir.

Hir sark suld be hir body nixt,
Of chestetie so quhyt,   10
With schame and dreid togidder mixt,
The same suld be perfyt.

Hir kirtill suld be of clene constance,
Lasit with lesum lufe,
The mailyeis of continuance
For nevir to remufe.

Hir gown suld be of gudliness,
Weill ribband with renowne,
Purfillit with plesour in ilk place,
Furrit with fyne fassoun.   20

Hir belt suld be of benignitie,
About hir middle meit;
Hir mantill of humilitie,
To thoill bayth wind and weit.

Hir hat suld be of fair having,
And hir tepat of trewth;
Hir patelet of gud pansing;
Hir hals ribbane of rewth.

Hir slevis suld be of esperance,
To keip hir fra dispair;   30
Hir gluvis of gud govirnance
To gyd hir fyngearis fair.

Hir schone suld be of sickernes,
In syne that scho nocht slyd;
Hir hoise of honestie, I ges,
I suld for hir provyd.

Wald scho put on this garmond gay,
I durst sweir by my seill,
That scho woir nevir grene nor gray
That set hir half so weill.   40

32

The Garment of Good Ladies

Would my good lady love me most,
And keep faith with me,
I should fine garments of the handsomest
Have made for her body.

Of high honour should be her hood,
Upon her head to wear,
Garnished with discretion so good,
No suspicion should she fear.

Her shift should be her body next,
Of chastity so white,   10
With shame and dread together mixed,
And the result should be just right.

Her kirtle should be of constancy,
Laced up with lawful love,
The eyelets of stability,
Them never to remove.

Her gown should be of goodliness,
Well ribboned with renown,
Trimmed with pleasure in every place,
Furred in fine fashion.   20

Her belt should be of benignity,
About her middle well set;
Her mantle of humility,
To suffer both wind and wet.

Her hat should be of a fair bearing,
Her tippet of things true;
Her partlet of good thinking;
Her neck ribbon of rue.

Her sleeves should be of hopefulness,
To keep her from despair;   30
 Her gloves of good discreteness,
To hide her fingers fair.

Her shoes should be of steadfastness,
In sin that she not slide;
Her hose of honesty, I guess,
I should for her provide.

Would she put on these garments gay,
I dare swear by my seal,
That she wore never green nor grey,
That became her half as well.   40

Notes

This poem is associated with the First Epistle of Paul to Timothy, Chapter 2, verses 9-11.

> 9 In like manner also, that women adorn themselves in modest apparel, with shamefacedness and sobriety; not with broided (braided) hair, or gold, or pearls, or costly array;
>
> 10 But (which becometh women professing godliness) with good works.
>
> 11 Let the woman learn in silence with all subjection.

Henryson seeks to robe 'the good lady' in graces and good virtues.

Line 5	hud (honour) – hood – a covering for the head, not attached to a cloak or coat.
Line 9	sark (chastity) – shift – a woman's shift or chemise, made of thin linen. It was T- shaped, with narrow sleeves and a wide neckline and was long in length.
Line 13	kirtill (constancy) – kirtle – a garment with both bodice and skirt. It held the shift in place and provided support for the bust. It had a wide neckline and tight short sleeves and was worn under the gown, laced tightly.
Line 17	gown (goodliness, renown) – the gown had a round low neckline or was v-necked, with a wide shallow collar. The bodice was tight and the skirt long. The fullness in the skirt was achieved by placement of gores as no pleating was used. Lacing was used to fasten the gown at the back. The gown was made of wool or silk and was trimmed with contrasting material.
Line 21	belt (benignity) – belts or girdles were worn round the waist by both men and women.
Line 23	mantill (humility) – mantels were similar to modern day capes. They consisted of large pieces of cloth of different sizes worn over both shoulders and fastened by cords or a button and a loop at the centre of the chest. They were hooded, sometimes with sleeves, and worn for protection against rain and cold.
Line 26	tepat (all things true) – tippet – a woman's tippet – an outdoor covering for the neck or neck and shoulders or a long strip hanging from the apex of the hood.
Line 27	patelet (good thinking) – a ruffle covering the throat and bust.
Line 33	schone (steadfastness) – shoes – made from leather from calf or goat skin. Wooden platforms called 'pattens' were strapped to the bottom of the shoes to protect them from mud.
Line 35	hoiss (honesty) – hose – knitted or cloth covering for the foot and part of the leg made of woven fabric, usually wool. The women's hose were knee length and were held up by garters.
Line 39	green – gaily coloured; grey – soberly coloured.

The Prais of Aige

The Prais of Aige

Within ane garth, undir a reid roseir,
Ane auld man and decrepit, hard I sing;
Gay was the not, sweit was the voce and cleir;
It was grit joy to heir of sic a thing.
And as me thocht, he said in his dyting,
'For to be yung I wald not, for my wiss
Of all this warld to mak me lord and King:
The moir of aige the nerrer hevynis bliss.

'Fals is this warld, and full of variance,
Besocht with syn and other sytis mo;   10
Trewth is all tynt, gyle hes the govirnance,
Wretchitness hes wrocht all weill to wo;
Fredome is tynt, and flemyt the lordis fro,
And covettyce is all the cause of thiss;
I am content that yowtheid is ago:
The moir of age the nerrer hevynis bliss.

'The stait of youth I repute for na gude,
For in that stait sic perilis now I see;
But speciall grace, the regeing of his blude
Can nane ganestand, quhill that he aigit be;   20
Syne of the thing befoir that joyit he
Nothing remanis now to be callit his;
For-why it was bot verry vanitie:
The moir of aige the nerrer hevynis bliss.

'Suld no man trust this wrechit world, for-quhy
Of erdly joy ay sorow is the end;
The stait of it can no man certify,
This day a king, to morne na thing to spend.
Quhat haif we heir bot grace us to defend?
The quhilk God grant us till mend our miss,   30
That to His gloir He ma our saulis send;
The moir of aige the nerrer hevynis bliss.'

Notes

Life on earth was seen as preparation for the afterlife. Heaven, Purgatory and Hell were all seen as real places and the main aim in being alive was to behave in such a way as to gain entry through Death's door to Heaven, to eternal bliss.

In this poem Henryson voices his displeasure with the state of the world and the behaviour of those in it. Sinning, lies, and greed beset the world. The passing years and age only bring the answer to problems caused by the passions of youth.

The nearer one was to heaven the closer one was to unencumbered bliss.

The Praise of Age

Within a garden, under a red rose-tree,
An old decrepit man I heard sing;
Gay the note, sweet and clear in voice sang he.
It was great joy to hear of such a thing.
And as I thought, he said in his singing,
'To be young again I would not wish
Even if all this world made me lord and king:
The older one is the nearer heaven's bliss.

'False is this world and full of variance,
Beset with sin and other sorrows so.   10
Truth is lost. Guile has the governance.
Wretchedness has brought all happiness to woe.
Generosity is lost, and the lords driven to go,
And covetousness is all the cause of this.
I am content that youth was long ago.
The older one is the nearer heaven's bliss.

'The state of youth I believe it holds no good,
For in that state such perils I now see.
Without special grace, the passion of his blood
Can none resist until he aged be;   20
Since of the thing before that enjoyed he
Nothing remains now to be called his
Because it were but very vanity.
The older one is the nearer heaven's bliss.

'No man should trust this wretched world, for why
Of earthly joy sorrow is always the end.
The state of it can no man certify.
This day a king. Tomorrow nothing to spend.
What have we here but grace us to defend?
The which God grant us to mend our ways,   30
That to His glory He may our souls send.
The older one is the nearer heaven's bliss.'

The Ressoning betwixt Aige and Youth

The Ressoning betwixt Aige and Youth

Youth.
Quhen fair Flora, the goddas of al flowris,
Baith firth and field freschly hed outfret,
And perly dropis of the balmy schowris
Thir wodis grene hed with the wattir wet,
Musand alone in mornyng I met
A mery man, that al of myrth cowd mene,
Syngand this sang that rycht swetly wess set:
'O youth, be glaid in to thi flowris grene.'

Aige.
I lukit furth a litill me befor,
And saw ane catyf one a club cumand,   10
With chekis leyne and lyart lokis hoir;
His eyne was hol, his voce wes hace hostand,
Walowit richt wan, waik as ane wand,
A bil he bure apone his brest abone,
In letteris leill but lyis, with this legyand,
'O youth, thi flowris fadis ferly sone.'

Youth.
This young man lap apone the land ful lycht,
And mervalit mekil of his makdome maid;
'Waldyne I am,' quod he, 'and wondir wycht,
With brawne as bair, with brest burle and braid;   20
No grume on ground my gardone may degraid,
Nor of my pytht may pair wyrtht half a prene;
My face is fair, my figour may nocht faid:
'O youth, be glaid in to thi flowris grene.'

Aige.
This senyour sang bot with a sobir stevyne
Schakand his berd, he said, 'My barne, let be;
I wes within thir sexty yeir and sevyne
A frek one fold, als fair, as frech, als fre,
Als glaid, als gay, als ying, als yaip as ye;
Bot now tha dayis ourdrevin are and done;   30
Luk thow my laythly lycome gyf I le:
'O youth, thi flowris fadis ferly sone.'

The Reasoning between Age and Youth

Youth.
When fair Flora, the goddess of all flowers,
Both woods and fields fresh with blooms had set,
And pearly drops of the balmy showers
The woodlands green had with their water wet,
Musing alone in the morning I met
A merry man, who only a diversion did mean,
Singing this song that really sweetly was set,
'O youth, rejoice in all your flowers green.'

Age.
I looked further a little space before,
And saw a wretch on a staff coming,   10
With cheeks lean and grey locks hoar;
His eyes were hollow, his voice, a hoarse hack
Withered really pale, as frail as any sapling.
A placard he bore upon his breast above,
An inscription, honest and true, stating,
'O youth, your flowers wither very soon.'

Youth.
This young man leapt upon the land full nimbly
And marveled much at the misjudgment made;
'Supple I am,' said he, 'and very sturdy,
With muscles like a boar and breast burly made;   20
No man on earth my prowess may degrade,
Nor of my virility may impair its worth half a pin;
My face is fair. My figure will not fade.
O youth, rejoice in all your flowers green.'

Age.
This old man sang, but with sad feeling,
Shaking his beard, he said, 'My child, let be;
I was within these sixty years and seven, living
As a foot soldier, as strong, as free,
As glad, as gay, as young, as active as ye;
But now those days are long past and done   30
Look at my loathly appearance. No lie you see.
O youth, your flowers wither very soon.'

Youth.
This mirrie man of mirth yit movit mair:
'My cors is clene without corruptioun,
My self is sauf fra seiknes and fra sair,
My wittis fyve in dew proportioun,
 My curage is of clene complexioun,
My hairt is haill, my levar, and my splene;
Thairfoir to reid this roll I haif no ressoun.
O youth, be glaid in to thi flowris grene.'   40

Aige
The bevar hoir said to the burlie berne:
'This brief thow sall abyd, sone be thow bald;
Thy strenth, thy stait, thocht it be stark and strene,
The feveris fell for eild, sal gar the fald;
Thy cors sall cling, thy curage sall wax cald,
Thy heill sall hink, and tak ane hurt bot bone,
Thy wittis fyve sall wane, thocht thow nocht wald:
O youth, thi yeiris faidis ferlie sone.'

Youth
Ane uthir verse this young man yit coud syng:
'At luffis law I think a quhil to leit   50
In court to cramp clenly in my clething,
And luk amang thir lusty ladeis sweit;
Of mariagis to mel with mowis meit,
In secretness, quhar we may nocht be sene,
And sa with birdis blythly my balis beit:
O youth, be glaid in to thi flowris grene.'

Aige
This awstrene greif ansuerit angirly:
'For thi cramping thow sall baith cruke and cowre;
Thy fleschely lust thow sall also defy,
And pane the sall put fra paramour;   60
Than will no bird be blyth of the in bouir;
Quhen thi manheid sall wendin as the mone,
Thow sall assay gif that my song be sour:
O youth, thi flowris fedis fellone sone.'

This galyart grutchit with sic grit greif,
He on his wayis wrethly went but wene;
This lene awld man luche not, bot tuk his leif,
And I abaid undir the levis grene:
Of the sedullis the suthe quhen I had sene,
Of trewth, me thocht, thay triumphit in thair toun: 70
'O youth, be glaid in to thi flowris grene!
O youth thi flowris faldis fellone sone!'

Youth.
This merry man of mirth yet went on more;
'My body is clean without corruption.
My state is sound, without sickness or sore,
My five wits in due proportion,
My temperament is of healthy condition
My heart is sound, my liver and my spleen;
Therefore to read this scroll I have no reason;
O youth, rejoice in all your flowers green.'   40

Age.
This hoary old man said to this burly gallant:
'This brief you shall obey, soon be you bald;
Your state, your strength, though it be strong and pliant,
The bad fevers and age shall gain the fold;
Your body shall shrivel, your spirit shall grow cold,
The health shall falter, and fail very soon.
Your five wits shall vanish, not long they hold;
O youth, your flowers wither very soon.'

Youth.
Another verse yet this young man could sing;
'At love's game I think a while to compete   50
In court to swagger well in my clothing,
And look among the comely ladies sweet,
Of marriages to deal with mouthings mete,
In privacy, where we may not be seen,
And so with ladies happily my lust beat;
O youth, rejoice in all your flowers green.'

Age.
This grave old man gave answer angrily;
'For your swaggering you shall become crooked and cower;
Your fleshly lust diminish speedily   60
And pain will ban you from your paramour;
Then will no lady be happy in the bower;
When your manhood shall wane like the moon,
You shall judge if my song is sour.
O youth, your flowers wither very soon.'

This gallant grumbled and began to grieve,
He on his way went angry, as it would be seen;
This lean old man laughed not, but took his leave.
And I stayed under the leaves green:
 Of the writings the sense which I had seen
Truly, I thought, they differed in their tune   70
'O youth, rejoice in all your flowers green!
O youth your flowers wither very soon!'

Notes

A poem similar to this was written in the fourteenth century. In it a youth goes out poaching in a wood. He wearies of the task and sits down to rest. Before him appear three men, a youth, a middle-aged man, and an old man. The youth's aim in life is to fight in a tournament to prove himself to his lady. The middle-aged man advises him instead to gain land, wealth and security. The old man, however, recognizes and states the inevitability of death and loss, the transitory nature of all things worldly, and the futility of the pleasures of youth and the prudence of middle age.

In 'The Reasoning between Age and Youth' only a youth and an old man appear. The youth says he is healthy, strong, virile, and fond of comely ladies. The old man tells him that as he grows older his strength will disappear, ill health will come, and his virility will diminish so that consorting with comely ladies will lead to nothing. They part in disagreement.

The Abbay Walk

The Abbay Walk

Allone as I went up and doun
In to ane abbay, fair to se,
Thinkand quhat consolatioun
Was best in to adversitie,
On caiss I kest on syd myne e,
And saw this writtin on a wall:
'Of quhat estait, man, that thow be,
Obey, and thank thy God of all.

'Thy kingdome and thy grit empyre,
Thy ryaltie, nor riche array,   10
Sall nocht endeur at Thy desyre,
Bot as the wind will wend away;
Thy gold and all thy gudis gay,
Quhen fortoun list will fra the fall;
Sen thow sic sampillis seis ilk day,
Obey, and thank thi God of all.

'Job wes maist riche, in Writ we find,
Thobe maist full of cheritie:
Job woux pure, and Thobe blynd,
Bath temptit with adversitie.   20
Sen blindness wes infirmitie,
And poverty wes naturall,
Rycht patiently bath he and he
Obeyid, and thankit God of all.

'Thocht thow be blind, or haif ane halt,
Or in thy face deformit ill,
Sa it cum nocht throw thy defalt,
Na man suld the repreif by skill.
Blame nocht thy Lord, sa is His will;
Spurn nocht thy fute aganis the wall;   30
Bot with meik hairt and prayer still
Obey, and thank thy God of all.

'God of His justice mon correct,
And of His mercy petie haif;
He is ane Juge to nane suspect,
To puneiss synfull man and saif.
Thocht thow be lord attour the laif,
And eftirwart maid bund and thrall,
Ane pure begger, with skrip and staif,
Obey, and thank thy God of all.   40

The Abbey Walk

Alone as I went up and down
In an abbey, which was fair to see,
Thinking what consolation
Was best in adversity,
By chance I did see near me
These instructions written upon a wall;
'Of what estate, man, that thou be,
Obey, and thank thy God for all.

'Thy kingdom and thy great empire,
Thy royalty or rich array   10
Shall not endure at thy desire
But as the wind will wend away;
Thy gold and all thy goods so gay,
When fortune chooses will from thee fall;
Since thou such instances see each day,
Obey, and thank thy God for all.

'Job was most rich, in scriptures we find,
Tobit most full of charity:
Job grew poor and Tobit blind,
Both tested with adversity.   20
Since blindness was infirmity,
And poverty was natural,
Therefore in patience both he and he
Obeyed, and thanked God for all.

'Though you be blind, even yet halt
Or in your face deformed ill,
If it came not through your fault,
No man should of you be critical.
Blame not your Lord, thus is His will;
Spurn not your foot against the wall;   30
But with meek heart and prayer still,
Obey, and thank thy God for all.

'God's justice leads Him to correct,
And by His mercy, pity to have;
He is a Judge, to none suspect,
To punish sinful man, and him to save.
Though you be lord above them all,
And afterwards made bound, in thrall,
A poor beggar with bag, staff and all
Obey, and thank thy God for all.   40

'This changeing and grit variance
Of erdly staitis up and doun
Is nocht bot casualitie and chance,
As sum men sayis without ressoun,
Bot be the grit provisioun
Of God aboif, that rewl the sall;
Thairfoir evir thow mak the boun
To obey, and thank thy God of all.

'In welth be meik, heich nocht thy self;
Be glaid in wilfull povertie;   50
Thy power and thy warldly pelf
Is nocht bot verry vanitie.
Remember Him that deit on the tre,
For thy saik taistit the bittir gall;
Quha heis law hairtis and lawis he;
Obey, and thank thy God of all.'

Notes

The Abbey mentioned may be Dunfermline Abbey.

Verse 3
It was believed at this time that God sent plagues, famine, disasters, and personal trials and tribulations as a means of showing his displeasure with mortals. If you sinned God would punish you. In verse three Henryson uses the experiences of Job and Tobit to illustrate that acceptance was the best reaction. Railing against God was not the answer.

The Book of Job Chapter 1, verses 1-22
Job was the 'greatest of all the men of the east.' He was rich and pious and stood well in the light of God. In one day his animals were stolen and his servants killed, his sheep, and those tending them,were struck by the fire of God, his camels were stolen and his camel men and his three young sons were killed. Job did not turn against God but said, 'The Lord gave and the Lord hath taken away; blessed be the name of the Lord.'

The Book of Tobias Chapter 13 verse 2
The Book of Tobias may be found in the Latin Vulgate Bible, which was translated at Douay-Rheims, towards the end of the 16th century, and forms part of the Old Testament. It was probably written about 175 B.C. It tells what happened to a good and pious man called Tobit and his son Tobias.

At one point Tobit became blind due to swallow dung falling into his eyes. He was resigned to his fate. He did not blame God for what had happened to him and went on behaving in the same way as he had before. Eventually with the help of his son Tobias he recovered his sight. He did not blame God for his personal suffering.

'This changing and great variance
Up and down of earthly position
Comes not by accident and chance,
As some men say, without reason,
But by the great provision
Of God above that rules the soul;
Therefore ever you make ready soon
To obey, and thank thy God for all.

'In wealth be meek, elevate not thyself;
Be glad in lonely poverty;   50
Thy power and thy worldly wealth
Is naught but very vanity.
Remember Him that died on a tree,
For thy sake tasted the bitter gall,
Who exalts humble hearts and brings down the lofty.
Obey, and thank thy God of all.'

The Ressoning betwix Deth and Man

The Ressoning betwix Deth and Man

Deth.
'O mortal man, behald, tak tent to me,
Quhilk suld thy mirrour be baith day and nicht;
All erdly thing that evir tuik lyfe mon de:
Paip, empriour, king, barroun, and knycht,
Thocht thay be in thair royall stait and hicht,
May nocht ganestand, quhen I pleise schute this derte;
Wal townis, castellis, and towiris, nevir so wicht,
May nocht resist quhill it be at his herte.'

Man.
'Now quhat art thow that biddis me thus tak tent,
And mak ane mirrour day and nicht of the   10
Or with thy dert I suld rycht sair repent?
I trest trewly of that thow sall sone le.
Quhat freik on fold sa bald dar manis me,
Or with me fecht, owthir on fute or horse?
Is non so wicht, or stark in this cuntre,
Bot I sall gar him bow to me on forse.'

Deth.
'My name, forsuth, sen that thow speiris,
Thay call me Deid, suthly I the declair,
Calland all, man and woman, to thair beiris,
Quhen-evir I pleise, quhat tyme, quhat place, or quhair?   20
Is nane sa stout, sa fresche, nor yit sa fair,
Sa yung, sa ald, sa riche, nor yit sa peur,
Quhair-evir I pass, owthir lait or air,
Mon put thame haill on forse undir my cure.'

Man.
'Sen it is so, that Nature can so wirk,
That yung and auld, with riche and peur, mon de,
In my youtheid, allace, I wes full irk,
Could not tak tent to gyd and governe me,
Ay gude to do, fra evill deidis to fle,
Trestand ay youtheid wald with me abyde,   30
Fulfilland evir my sensualitie
In deidly syn, and specialy in pryd.'

The Reasoning between Death and Man

Death.
'O mortal man, pay attention to me,
Who should your mirror be both day and night;
All earthly thing that ever took life must die:
Pope, emperor, king, baron, and knight,
Though they be in their royal state and might,
May not withstand, when I choose to shoot this dart;
Walled towns, castles, and towers of great height,
May not stop the dart till it reach his heart.'

Man.
'Now what are you that bids me be intent,
And make a mirror day and night of thee?   10
Or with your dart I should really sore repent?
I trust that you do lie of this, truly.
What creature on earth would dare menace me,
Or with me fight, either on foot or horse?
There is none so strong, or fierce in this country,
But I shall make him bow to me by force.'

Death.
'My name, in truth, since me you are asking,
They call me Death, truly I you declare,
Calling all men and women to their burying,
Whenever I please, what time, what place, or where.   20
There is none so stout, so fresh, nor yet so fair,
So young, so old, so rich, nor yet so needy,
Where ever I pass, either late or early,
But must submit themselves to me completely.'

Man.
'Since it is so, that Nature is thus intent,
That young and old, with rich and poor, must die,
In my youth, alas, I was indifferent,
Did not take care to guide and control me,
Always good to do, from evil deeds to flee,
Trusting youth would always with me abide,   30
Satisfying ever my sensuality
In deadly sin, and especially in pride.'

Deth.
'Thairfoir repent and remord thy conscience;
Think on thir wordis I now upoun the cry:
O wrechit man! O full of ignorance!
All thy plesance thow sall richt deir aby;
Dispone thy-self and cum with me in hy,
Edderis, askis, and wormis meit for to be;
Cum quhen I call, thow ma me not deny,
Thocht thow war Paip, Empriour, and King, all thre.'   40

Man.
'Sen it is swa fra the I may not chaip,
This wrechit warld for me heir I defy,
And to the deid, to lurk under thy caip,
I offer me with hairt richt humily;
Beseiking God, the divill, myne ennemy,
No power haif my sawill till assay.
Jesus, on The, with peteous voce, I cry,
Mercy on me to haif on domis day.'

Notes

Death in the middle ages was an everyday experience, always close at hand as a result of the
conditions at the time. Disease flourished due to the lack of effective medicine and ill-informed
diagnosis. Hygiene was rudimentary and many babies died during the early stages of life
while children succumbed to infection and childhood diseases. Famine was not an unusual
occurrence. War and strife led to many deaths, both in battle and in its following consequences.
Thoughts about dying filled the minds of the living. Death was seen as the gateway to Heaven,
Purgatory, and Hell, the allocated destination depending on the purity of life led and the
formalities required when dying.
A 'good' death required administration of the Last Rites, which included confession, and final
forgiveness.
A 'bad' death was caused by the lack of the confession of sins and no absolution, the soul being
consigned to purgatory or hell for eternity.
In the poem Henryson states the inevitability of death and expresses the fear that his behaviour
in the days of his youth will make him fare ill after his death. He tries to challenge Death but
Death remains remorseless saying he comes for everyone.
Henryson hopes that God will be merciful to him and that Jesus will save him from the Devil
on Doomsday.

Death.
'Therefore repent and examine your conscience;
Think on these words I now upon you cry;
O wretched man! O full of ignorance!
All your pleasures you shall dearly buy;
Prepare yourself and come with me, come hie,
Adders', newts', and worms' meat to be;
Come when I call, you may not me deny,
Though you were pope, emperor, and king, all three.'   40

Man.
'Since this is so I may not from you escape,
I renounce this wretched world for me,
And to the death, to wait in a coffin cape,
I offer myself truly, really humbly;
Beseeching God that the Devil, my enemy,
No power has my soul to assay.
Jesus, on Thee, with piteous voice I cry,
To have mercy on me on Doomsday.'

Aganis Haisty Credence of Titlaris

Aganis Haisty Credence of Titlaris

Fals titlaris now growis up full rank,
Nocht ympit in the stok of cheretie,
Howping at thair lord to gett grit thank;
Thay haif no dreid on thair nychtbouris to lie;
Than suld ane lord awyse him weill and se,
Quhen ony taill is brocht to his presence,
Gif it be groundit in to veretie,
Or he thairto gif haistily creddence.

Ane worthy lord suld wey ane taill wyslie,
The taill-tellar, and quhome of it is tald;   10
Gif it be said for luve, or for invy,
And gif the taillis-man abyd at it he wald;
Than eftirwart the pairteis suld be cald
For thair excuse to mak lawfull defence:
Than suld ane lord the ballance evinly hald,
And gif not at the first haistie creddence.

It is no wirschep for ane nobill lord,
For fals taillis to put ane trew man doun,
And, gevand creddence to the first record,
He will not heir his excusatioun;   20
The tittillaris so in his eir can roun,
The innocent may get no audience;
Ryme as it may, thair is na ressoun
To gif till taillis haistily creddence.

Thir taill-tellaris oft tymes dois grit skaith,
And raissis mortall feid and discrepance,
And makis lordis with thair servandis wraith,
And baneist be withoutin cryme perchance.
It is the grund of stryf and all distance,
Moir perrellus than ony pestillence,   30
Ane lord in flatterreris to haif plesance,
Or to gif lyaris hestely creddence.

O thow wyse lord, quhen that a flatterer,
The for to pleise, and hurt the innocent,
Will tell a taill of thy familiar,
Thow suld the pairteis call incontinent,
And sitt doun sadly in to jugement,
And serche the cause weill, or thow gif sentence,
Or ellis heireftir, perchance thow may repent,
That thow to taillis gaif so grit creddence.   40

Against Hasty Credence of Tattlers

False tattlers now grow up full rank,
Not grafted in the stalk of charity,
Hoping from their lord to get great thank;
To lie about their neighbours no fear, have they.
Then should a lord bethink himself well and see,
When any tale is brought to his presence,
Whether it be grounded in verity,
Before he thereto gives hastily credence.

A worthy lord should weigh a tale wisely,
The tale-teller, and of whom it is told;   10
If it be said for love or for envy,
And if the tale-teller will to his story hold;
Then afterwards the parties should be called
For their evidence to make lawful defence:
Then should the lord the balance evenly hold,
And judge not at the first hasty credence.

It is no honour for a noble lord,
To put a good man down by accusation,
And giving credence to the first record,
He will not hear his explanation;   20
In his ear, the tattlers pour their version,
While the innocent may get no audience;
Sound as it may, there is no reason,
Hastily to give to tales credence.

These tale-tellers often do great injury,
And raise mortal feud and discrepance,
And make lords with their servants angry,
And banish them without a crime perchance.
It is the ground of strife and discordance,
More perilous than any pestilence,   30
A lord in flatterers to have pleasance,
Or to give hastily to liars, credence.

O thou wise lord, when that a flatterer
You to please, and to hurt the innocent,
Will tell a tale of about a person to you familiar,
You should the parties call at that moment,
And sit down soberly to make a judgment,
And look for the cause well, before sentence,
Or else hereafter, perchance you may repent
That to tales you gave such credence.   40

O wicket tung, sawand dissentioun,
Of fals taillis to tell that will not tyre,
Moir perrellus than ony fell poysoun,
The pane of hell thow sall haif to thi hyre.
Richt swa thay sall that hes joy or desyre
To gife his eir to heir with patience;
For of discord it kendillis mony fyre,
To gif talis ovir haistie creddence,

Bakbyttaris to heir it is no bourd,
For thay ar excommunicat in all place;   50
Thre personis severall he slayis with ane wourd –
Him-self, the heirar, and the man saiklace.
Within ane hude he hes ane doubill face,
Ane bludy tung, undir a fair pretence.
I say no moir; bot God grant lordis grace,
To gif to taillis nocht hestely creddence.

Notes

| Line 1 | titlaris – tattlers, tale tellers, gossips. |

One of Solomon's proverbs warns against becoming a 'titlar': 'Beware of useless murmuring and keep your tongue from slander, because no secret word is without result, and a lying mouth destroys the soul'.

The poem warns those who listen to 'titlars' of the dangers in doing so.

Line 1-2   'nocht ympit' – not engrafted.

'full rank' – as weeds.

Horticultural imagery has been used, i.e. the plant which is engrafted to a good stalk will be productive, unlike the weeds which grow in unruly and unwanted profusion.' False tale-tellers are growing like weeds, devoid of any goodness.

Line 23   Proverb –   Manie man maks ryme and luikes to no reason.'

'Many men speak nonsense.' (Proverbs in Scots – James Carmichaell)

Line 54   'bludy' – used abusively.

O wicked tongue, sowing dissension,
Of false tales to tell that will not tire,
More perilous than any bad poison,
The pain of hell you shall have as your hire.
Just as they shall who have joy or desire
To give their ear to hear with patience:
For of discord it lights many a fire,
Through giving tales hasty credence.

To hear backbiters it is no trivial thing,
For they are accursed in every place;   50
With a word three persons separately slaying –
Himself, the hearer, and the man guiltless.
Hidden in a hood he has a double face,
A bloody tongue under a fair pretence.
I say no more; but God grant lords grace,
To not give tales hastily credence.

The Annunciation

The Annunciation

Forcy as deith is likand lufe,
Throuch quhom al bittir swet is.
No thing is hard, as Writ can pruf,
Till him in lufe that letis;
Luf us fra barret betis;
Quhen fra the hevinly sete abufe,
In message Gabriell couth muf,
And with mild Mary metis,
And said, 'God wele the gretis;
In thee He will tak rest and rufe   10
But hurt of syne, or yit reprufe:
In Him sett thi decretis.'

This message mervale gert that Myld,
And silence held but soundis,
As weill aferit, a maid infild,
The angell it expoundis,
How that hir wame but woundis
Consave it suld, fra syne exild.
And quhen this carpin wes compild
Brichtnes fra bufe aboundis;   20
Than fell that gay to groundis,
Of Goddis grace na thing begild,
Wox in hir chaumer chaist with child,
With Christ our King that crownd is.

Thir tithingis tauld, the Messinger
Till hevin agane he glidis:
That princes pure, withoutyn peir.
Full plesandly applidis,
And blith with barne abidis.
O worthy wirship singuler,   30
To be moder and madyn meir,
As Cristin faith confidis;
That borne was of hir sidis,
Our Maker, Goddis Sone, so deir,
Quhilk erd, wattir, and hevinnis cler,
Throw grace and virtu gidis.

The Annunciation

Forceful as death is pleasing love,
Through which all bitter sweet is.
No thing is hard as writ can prove
To him in love that brought is.
Love from contention keeps us.
When from the heavenly seat above,
Messenger Gabriel did move
And with mild Mary he meets
And said, 'God well you greets.
In thee He will rest and repose.   10
Without reproof or any sin.
Surrender your will to Him.'

This message awed that Mary mild,
And caused her to make no sounds
As behoves a maid undefiled.
The angel it then expounds
How that her womb without wounds
Conceive it should, from sin preserved.
When this message was completed
Light did from above abound: 20
Then fell Mary to the ground,
By God's grace in no way beguiled,
Grew, in her chamber, chaste, with child,
With Christ, our King, that crowned is.

These tidings told, the messenger
Unto heaven again he glides:
That princess pure, without a peer,
Full agreeably inclined is,
And gladly with child abides.
O worthy worship singular,   30
To be mother and maiden pure,
As the Christian faith makes clear;
That born of her womb was
Our Maker, God's Son, oh so dear,
Who earth, and water, and heavens clear,
Through both grace, and virtue guides.

The miraclis ar mekle and meit,
Fra luffis ryver rynnis;
The low of luf haldand the hete
Unbrynt full blithlie birnis;   40
Quhen Gabriell beginnis
With mouth that gudely May to grete,
The wand of Aarone, dry but wete,
To burioun nocht blynnis;
The flesch all donk within is,
Upone the erd na drop couth fleit;
Sa was that May maid Moder swete,
And sakeles of all synnis.

Hir mervalus haill madinhede
God in hir bosum bracis,   50
And hir divinite fra deid
Hir kepit in all casis.
The Hie God of His gracis
Him-self dispisit us to speid,
And dowtit nocht to dee one deid:
He panit for our peacis,
And with His blude us bacis;
Bot quhen He ras up, as we rede,
The cherite of His Godhede
Was plane in every placis.   60

O Lady lele and lusumest,
Thy face moist fair and schene is!
O blosum blithe and bowsumest,
Fra carnale cryme that clene is!
This prayer fra my splene is,
That all my werkis wikkitest
Thow put away, and mak me chaist
Fra Termigant that teyn is,
And fra his cluke that kene is;
And syne till hevin my saule thou haist,   70
Quhar thi Makar of michtis mast
Is King, and thow thair Quene is.

These miracles are many and mete,
Which from love's river yet runs;
The fire of love holding the heat,
Unburnt, full blythly it burns.   40
When Gabriel he begins
By word that goodly maid to greet,
The staff of Aarone, dry complete,
Burgeons and to grow begins.
The flesh, all moist, within is,
Yet no drop the earth did meet.
So was that maid made Mother sweet,
Who innocent of sin is.

Her marvellous perfect maidenhead
God in her womb encloses   50
And her divinity from deed
She kept safe in all cases.
The high God of His graces
To raise us, Himself He humbled,
And to die in fact naught doubted.
For all our peace He suffered,
And with His blood moistens us,
But when He rose up, as we read,
The charity of his Godhead
Was present in all places.   60

O Lady loyal and loveliest!
Your face most fair and bright is!
O blossom, blithe and buxomest,
From carnal sin that clean is!
This prayer from my heart is,
That all my works the wickedest
You put away, and make me guiltless
Safe from the termigant that fierce is,
And from his grip that keen is,
And then to heaven my soul you haste,   70
Where the maker of power greatest
Is King, and you their Queen is.

Notes

Verse 1	Gabriel was one of the seven great archangels. He appears four times in the scriptures, each time as a heavenly messenger. To Mary he announced the incarnation of Jesus Christ (Luke Chapter 1, verses 26-38).
Line 12	decretis – decisions.
Verse 4	Lines 40-48 – manifestations of several of God's interventions and/or presence on earth are referred to in this verse.

'unbrynt full blithlie birnis' – God spoke to Moses from a burning bush telling him that he would lead the children of Israel to the Promised Land. (Exodus Chapter 3, verses 1-4, 17)

God's message that Mary would give birth to God's son came to her by means of Gabriel.

'The wand of Aarone, dry but wete,' – Aaron's dry staff was placed overnight, along with others, 'in the tabernacle of the congregation' and his alone sprouted miraculously. This was taken as a sign from God that he was to be in charge of the tabernacle. (Numbers Chapter 17, verse 8)

Aaron's barren staff sprouted. Mary's undefiled barren womb conceived through God's intervention.

'The flesch all donk within is.' – Gideon sought a sign from God that He wanted Gideon to save Israel by leading the men of Israel into battle. He placed a dry fleece on the floor overnight. The next morning the fleece was moist but the floor around was dry. This event matched the sign that he was looking for and was his answer from God. (Judges Chapter 6, verse 37)

'So was that May maid moder suete.' – Mary was made 'mother sweet' by God's direct intervention, bearing a child, untouched.

Line 68	'termigant' – the name for a false god supposedly worshipped by the Saracens but used here as a name for the devil/s who tormented sinners in hell.

Sum Practysis of Medecyne

Sum Practysis of Medecyne

Guk, guk, gud day, Schir, gaip quhill ye get it,
Sic greting may gane weill gud laik in your hude
Ye wald deir me, I trow, because I am dottit,
To ruffill me with a ryme; na, Schir, be the rude,
Your saying I haif sene, and on syde set it,
As geir of all gaddering, glaikit, nocht gude;
Als your medicyne by mesour I haif meit, met it,
The quhilk, I stand ford, ye nocht understude,
Bot wrett on as ye culd to gar folk wene;
For feir my longis wes flaft,   10
Or I wes dottit or daft,
Gife I can ocht or the craft.
Heir be it sene.

Becaus I ken your cunnyng in to cure
Is clowtit and clampit and nocht weill cleird,
My prettik in pottingary ye trow be als pure,
And lyk to your lawitnes, I schrew thame that leid;
Is nowdir fevir, nor fell, that our the feild fure,
Seiknes nor sairness, in tyme gif I seid,
Bot I can lib thame and leiche thame fra lame and lesure,   20
With sawis thame sound mak: On your saule beid,
That ye be sicker of this sedull I send yow,
With the suthfast seggis,
That glean all egeis,
With dia and dreggis.
Of malis to mend yow.

Dia Culcakit

Cape cukmaid and crop the colleraige,
Ane medecyne for the maw, and ye cowth mak it,
With sweit satlingis and sowrokis, the sop of the sege,
The crud of my culume with your teith crakit   30
Lawrean and linget seid, and the luffage,
The hair of the hurcheoun nocht half deill hakkit,
With the snout of ane selch, ane swelling to swage;
This cure is callit in our craft Dia Culcakkit.
Put all thir in ane pan, with pepper and pik,
Syne sottin to this,
The count of ane sow kiss,
Is nocht bettir, I wiss.
For the collik

Some Practices of Medicine

Foolish fool! Good day, sir! Gape until you get it.'
Such greeting may suit well 'the lack in your hood'.
You would harm me, I believe, because I am of low wit,
To ruffle me with a rhyme; no, sir, by the rood (cross),
Your advice I have seen, and on side set it,
As nonsense all gathered, foolish, not good;
Also your medicine by measure I have judged it,
The which, I warrant, you nothing understood,
But wrote as you did to make folk believe it;
For fear my lungs were palpating   10
Or that I was stupid or lacking,
If I know of the craft anything,
Here will you see it.

Because I know your skill in finding a cure
Is so clumsy and botched, with no clarity in it,
My practice in pharmacy you believe is also poor,
And like your ignorance. I curse them who said it.
There is neither fever nor injury on the field for sure,
Sickness or disease, if in time I see it
But I can cut them and cure them from lameness and hurt, 20
With salves them make sound. On your soul be it
That you be certain of prescriptions I send you
To reliable apothecaries,
Who allay illness
With mixtures and drugs,
From sickness to mend you.

Dia Culcakit – Prescription for colic

Take excrement and gather the colleraige
A medicine for the stomach, and you could make it,
With dregs of wine and sorrel, the sap of the sage,
The curds of my fundament, with your pestle cracked;   30
Laurel and linseed, and the lovage,
The hair of the hedgehog somewhat chopped,
With the snout of a seal, a swelling to assuage;
This cure is called in our craft the drug for buttocks befouled.
Put all this in a pan with pepper and pitch
Then add into this,
The pudenda of a sow,
There is nothing better than this
For the colic.

Dia Longum

Recipe, thre ruggis of the reid ruke,   40
The gant of ane gray meir, the claik of ane guse,
The dram of ane drekterss, the douk of an duke,
The gaw of ane grene dow, the leg of ane louse,
Fyve unce of ane fle wing, the fyn of ane fluke,
With ane sleiffull of slak, that growis in the sluss;
Ming all thir in ane mass with the mone cruke.
This untment is rycht ganand for your awin uss,
With reid nettill seid in strang wesche to steip,
For to bath your ba cod
Quhen ye wald nop and nod;   50
Is nocht bettir, be God,
To latt yow to sleip

Dia Glaconicon

This dia is rycht deir and denteit in daill,
Cause it is trest and trew, thairfoir that ye tak
Sevin sobbis of ane selche, the quhidder of ane quhaill,
The lug of ane lempet is nocht to forsaik,
The harnis of ane haddok, hakkit or haill,
With ane bustfull of blude of the scho-bak,
With ane brewing caldrun full of hait caill,
For it wil be softar and sweittar of the smak   60
Thair is nocht sic ane lechecraft fra Lawdian to Lundin:
It is clippit in our cannon,
Dia Glacolicon,
For till fle awaye fon,
Quhair fulis ar fundin.

Dia Custrum.

The ferd feisik is fyne, and of ane felloun pryce,
Gud for haising, and hosting, or heit at the hairt;
Recipe. Thre sponfull of the blak spyce,
With ane grit gowpene of the gowk fart;
The lug of ane lyoun, the guse of ane gryce;   70
Ane unce of ane oster poik at the nether parte,
Annoyntit with nurice doung, for it is rycht nyce,
Myngit with mysdirt and with mustart;
Ye may clamp to this cure and ye will mak cost,
Bayth the bellox of ane brok,
With thre crawis of the cok
The schadow of ane yule stok
Is gud for the host.

Dia Longum - A lengthy prescription for (genital itch and)
sleeplessness.

Take three tugs of the red rook,   40
The yawn of a grey mare, the cry of a goose,
The dram of a drake's penis, the quack of one duck,
The gall of a green dove, the leg of a louse
Five ounce of a fly's wing, of the flounder a fin,
With one sieve full of seaweed, that grows in the ooze.
All this at the waning of the moon, mix right in.
This ointment is really suitable for your own use,
With red nettle seed in strong urine to steep,
To bathe your ball sack,
When you would nod and nap.
By God there is nothing you will lack
To help you to sleep   50

Dia Glaconicon -   Prescription for foolishness and folly .

This cure is expensive and does small portions entail,
As a result, it is trusted and true. Therefore you take
Seven sobs of a seal, the spouting of a whale,
The ear of a limpet you should not forsake,
The brains of a haddock, chopped or whole,
A jarful of blood of the she bat take
With a brewing cauldron full of hot kale,
For it will be the softer and will sweeter it make.   60
There is not such a remedy from Lothian to Lundin;
It is called in our canon
Dia Glacolicon,
That gets rid of folly soon,
Which fools abound in.

Dia Custrum - Prescription for rogues and the cough

The fourth physic is fine and of a high price,
Good for hoarseness, and coughing or burning at the heart.
Take three spoonfuls of the black spice,
With a great double handful of the cuckoo fart,
The ear of a lion, the long gut of a young pig,   70
An ounce bag of oyster at the nether part,
Anointed with nurse dirt, for it is right nice
Mixed with mouse dirt and with mustard.
You may add to this cure to give sustenance,
Both the testicles of a brock,
With three crows of the cock,
The shadow of a cabbage stalk,
Is good for the cough.

Gud nycht, guk, guk, for sa I began
I haif na come at this tyme langer to tary   80
Bot luk on this letter, and leird, gif ye can,
The prectik and poyntis of this pottingary;
Schir, minister this medecyne at evin to sum man,
And or pryme be past, my powder I pary,
Thay sall bliss yow, or ellis bittirly yow ban;
For it sall fle thame, in faith, out of the fary:
Bot luk quhen ye gaddir thir gressis and gerss,
Outhir sawrand or sour,
That it be in ane gud oure:
It is ane mirk mirrour   90
Ane uthir manis erss.

Good night cuckoo, for so I began,
I have no leisure at this time longer to tarry,   80
But look on this letter and learn if you can
The practice and points of this apothecary;
Sir, give this medicine at even to some man
And before sunrise be past, my powder I parry,
They shall bless you, or else bitterly you curse,
For it will drive them mad, making them crazy
Take care when you gather these herbs and grass
Either savoury or sour
That it be in a good hour:
'It is a dark mirror,   90
Another man's arse.'

Improvements in health were being made in Scotland during the 15th and 16th centuries. Regulations to prevent the spread of infectious diseases appear in the records of the Town Council of Edinburgh, e.g. in 1494 various regulations were laid down in respect of the sale of poultry, geese, flesh and other corruptible kinds of food.

King James IV (1473-1513) was very interested in medical matters and he influenced many of the changes which were made. He had a great deal of knowledge of medical practice and was also a good surgeon, so good in fact that his advice was sought from all over his realm. (Source – Lindesay of Pitscottie, *Cronicles of Scotland*) Apothecaries in the 15th century, who were often also barber surgeons, had a great deal of knowledge about the effects and uses of a wide variety of plants, animals and minerals and in dispensing their prescriptions would often use a considerable number of ingredients. One prescription called 'treacle' contained 60 ingredients, took 40 days to make and was allowed to mature for 12 years.

Some apothecaries were prone to using long and imposing prescriptions. In 'Some Practices of Medicine' Robert Henryson satirises the apothecaries and their prescriptions. It may be that Henryson was simply trying to deflate the apothecaries' opinions of themselves. On the other hand it was reported by the poet and courtier Sir Francis Kinaston (1587-1642) that 'being old Henryson died of a diarrhea, or flux' so the poem may reflect Henryson's dissatisfaction with his own treatment. The poem is very different from Henryson's other works and it may have been written in his later years.

The poem addresses directly an apothecary or apothecaries with verses three to six giving details of prescriptions. In verse three, most of the ingredients described were used by apothecaries although some in later verses appear of doubtful use in healing and have been included tongue in cheek.

Line 1	'Gaip quhill ye get it' – 'Your jaw will drop, your mouth open like a cuckoo waiting to be fed, when you hear what I am going to say' or 'keep your mouth open and take your medicine'.
Line 2	'laik in your hood' – 'There is good sport in your hood' – you are ludicrous.
Line 20	'Bot I can lib them' – 'lib' – cut or castrate.
Line 24	'That glean all egeis' – there are two interpretations of this:
	(1) which cure all illnesses.
	(2) who exhibit good practice using eggs to bind and hold other ingredients.
Verse 3	Dia Culcakit: Dia- signifies prescription; cul- faeces; cakit- caked – a purgative medicine.
Line 30	teith (pestle) – a name given to instrument used for pounding ingredients. Literally this may be the teeth.
Line 27-37	Ingredients:
	excrement – to cure sore throats, colic, cancer, cataract, baldness.
	colleraige – to cure obstructions, colds, swellings, bruises.
	sage – to cure epilepsy, intestinal worms, chest ailments.
	sorrel – to cure epidemics, stomach troubles.
	pitch – to cure wounds, ulcers, burns, scalds.
	resin – to cure pains in the joints.

	laurel – to cure fever, flux, gout, respiratory diseases, skin diseases, stomach problems.
	linseed – to cure kidney disease, constipation.
	lovage – to cure asthma, dropsy, gout, snake bites, sore throats, stomach troubles. Used also as a love potion.
Verse 4	Dia Longum: Dia- prescription, Longum- (1) lengthy; (2) genital itch?
Line 46	'with the mone cruk' – at the time of the crescent or waning moon, a time when the dews thought to be distilled from the moon were associated with facilitating magic.
Line 49	red nettle – used to cure itchy skin, rheumatism, impetigo.
Verse 5	Dia Glaconicon: Dia- prescription Glaconicon- glacach (gaelic) boil or swelling.
	This prescription claims to cure fools and foolishness. The source word within the prescription name 'glacach' is used to signify the symptoms of those who suffer from the disease much as the words boil, excrescence or wart are used nowadays describing those who display similar symptoms as fools. The word 'glaikit' – foolish – may come from the same source word.
Line 61	Lundin – the Lundin estate near Dunfermline, which lay directly opposite Lothian (north/south direction).
Verse 6	Dia Custrum: Dia- prescription, Custrum- rogue (Henryson's apothecary)
Line 71	oyster – had an aphrodisiac effect.
Line 71	'An ounce bag of oyster at the nether part' – a later cure for the colic was the placing a small bag or poke of warm herbs on the perineum to give relief. This prescription suggests placing a bag of oyster in a similar position, perhaps giving the resulting effect of an aphrodisiac or merely providing soothing heat to internal organs.
Line 73	mustard – used to cure gouts, stings, had aphrodisiac effects.
Line 72	'nurse dirt' – asafoetida or aloes applied to the breast to wean children.
	'yule stok' – winter cabbage or kale – used at Christmas and Hallowe'en.
Line 84	'pary' – wager.
Line 86	'out of the fary' – out of the illusion.
Lines 91-92	'That it be in a good time' – in order to ensure medicinal effects apothecaries collected their ingredients at certain times of the day and according to the position of the moon. It was believed that the strength and virtue of herbs was increased greatly by the position of celestial bodies during the period 23rd March to 23rd June.
Lines 91-2	These lines use a modified version of the proverb, which may be found in James Carmichaell's Proverbs in Scots: 'It is a mirk mirrour in my eie an other mans thocht', i.e. It is a mystery to me another man's thought. Henryson has used his own version to point out that the workings of his bowel remain a mystery to other men and seemingly in particular to his apothecary.

The Thre Deid Pollis

The Thre Deid Pollis

O sinfull man! in to this mortal se
Quhilk is the vaill of murning and of cair,
With gaistly sicht, behold our heidis thre
Our holkit ene, our peilit pollis bair;
As ye ar now, into this warld we wair,
Als fresche, als fair, als lusty, to behald.
Quhan thow lukis on this suth examplair
Of thy self, man, thow may be richt unbald.

For suth it is, that every man mortall
Mon suffer deid, and de, that lyfe hes tane;   10
Na erdly stait aganis deid ma prevaill;
The hour of deth and place is uncertane,
Quilk is referrit to the Hie God allane;
Heirfoir haif mynd of deth, that thow mon de;
This sair exampill to se quotidiane,
Suld cause all men fra wicket vycis fle.

O wanton yowth, als fresche as lusty May,
Farest of flowris, renewit quhyt and reid,
Behald our heidis: O lusty gallandis gay,
Full laichly thus sall ly thy lustyheid,   20
Holkit and how, and wallowit as the weid,
Thy crampand hair, and eik thy cristall ene,
Full cairfully conclud sall dulefull deid;
Thy example heir be us it may be sene.

O Ladies quhyt, in claithis corruscant,
Poleist with perle, and mony pretius stane;
With palpis quhyt, and hals so elegant,
Circulit with gold, and sapheris mony ane;
Your fingaris small, quhyt as quhailis bane,
Arrayit with ringis, and mony rubeis reid: 30
As we ly thus, so sall ye ly ilk ane,
With peilit polis, and holkit thus your heid.

O wofull pryd! the rute of all distres,
With humill hairt upoun our pollis penss:
Man, for thy miss, ask mercy with meikness;
Aganis deid na man may mak defenss,
The Empriour, for all his excellens,
King and Quene, and eik all erdly stait,
Peure and riche, sal be but differens,
Turnit in ass, and thus in erd translait.   40

The Three Dead Heads

O sinful man, in the light of spiritual struggle
Which is the valley of despondency and care,
With terror-stricken eyes behold our heads three,
Our hollowed-out eyes, our skinned skulls bare:
As you are now, in this world we were,
As fresh, as fair, as lusty to behold;
When you look on this true exemplar
Of yourself, man, you may be full of fear.

For truth it is, that every man mortal
Must suffer death, and die, who life has known.   10
No earthly state against death may prevail.
The hour and place of death is unknown,
Being known to the High God alone.
From now have mind of death that you must die;
This spectacle that is daily shown,
Should cause all men from wicked vice to fly.

O wanton youth, as fresh as beautiful May,
Fairest of flowers, grown new white and red,
Behold our heads: oh lusty gallant gay,
Full lowly thus shall lie your lusty head,   20
Hollowed and empty and as the weed quite dead,
Your curled hair, and also your crystal eyes;
Shall in doleful death, full sadly end.
Your example here, in us, now it lies.

O ladies white, in clothes coruscant,
Adorned with pearls and many a precious stone;
With breasts white, and necks so elegant,
Circled with gold, with sapphires sown.
Your fingers small, white as whales' bone,
Arrayed with rings and many rubies red.   30
As we lie thus, so shall you lie each alone,
With naked skulls and empty thus your head.

O woeful pride, the root of all distress,
Upon our skulls think with deference:
Man for your sins ask mercy with meekness;
Against death no man may make defence.
The emperor for all his excellence,
King and queen and also all earthly states,
Poor, rich, there will be no difference,
Turned into ash and thus to dust translates.   40

This questioun, quha can absolve, lat see,
Quhat phisnamour, or perfyt palmester –
Quha was farest, or fowlest, of us thre?
Or quhilk of us of kin was gentillar?
Or maist excellent in science, or in lare,
In art, musik, or in astronomye?
Heir suld be your study and repair,
And think, as thus all your heidis mon be.

O febill aige, ay drawand neir the dait
Of dully deid, and hes thy dayis compleit,   50
Behald our heidis with murning and regrait;
Fall on thy kneis; ask grace at God greit,
With orisionis, and haly psalmis sweit,
Beseikand Him on the to haif mercy,
Now of our saulis byand the decreit
Of His Godheid, when He shall call and cry.

Als we exhort, that every man mortall,
For His saik that maid of nocht all thing,
For our saulis to pray in general
To Jesus Chryst, of hevin and erd the King   60
That throwch His blude we may ay leif and ring
With the Hie Fader, be eternitie,
The Sone alswa, the Haly Gaist conding,
Thre knit in Ane be perfyt Unity.

This question, who can answer it let us see,
What physiognomist, or trained palmist,
Who was the fairest, or foulest of we three?
Or which of us the noblest?
Or most excellent as teacher or scientist,
In arts, music or astronomy?
Here should be your study and interest,
And think, as thus, all your heads must be.

O feeble age, drawing near the date
Of sorrowful death, and as your days complete,   50
Behold our heads with mourning and regret;
Fall on your knees; ask grace from God great,
With orations and holy psalms sweet,
Beseeching Him on thee to have mercy,
Now of our souls, awaiting the decree
Of His Godhead, when He does us glorify.

Also we exhort that every man mortal,
For His sake that made, of nothing, everything,
For our souls to pray in general
To Jesus Christ, of heaven and earth the King   60
That through His blood we may live, reigning
With the High Father, for eternity,
The Son also, the Holy Ghost condign (worthy),
Three combined in One by perfect Unity.

Notes

The theme of 'three talking dead' was common in illustrations during medieval times. The example in 'De Lisle Psalter' contains a picture of a group of three princes in all their finery in a meeting with three worm-eaten corpses who warn the princes that they will soon be cadavers, moldering and decaying as they are, their lives and finery seen as nothing. The imagery of the three dead heads is used in Henryson's poem to point out the frailty of life, the need for repentance, and the necessity for prayers for the souls of the dead awaiting in purgatory. It did not matter what your station in life was, how you looked or behaved, repentance and prayer was essential to save all souls.

Line 25   coruscant – giving out sparkles of light.

Line 42   physiognomist - one who judges human character from facial features.

The appearance of facial features is reliant on the structure of the skull i.e. on the bones of the cranium and facial bones. The facial construct is affected by the position of the cavities for the eyes, internal ears, and nose as well as the size and position of the upper and lower jaw bones, cheek bones, and the nose bone.

Examples of Judgements.

A person with a high brow indicates nobility, intelligence.
A low brow indicates dullness, criminality.

When a head in profile is longer than it is wide, with straight edged contours, this indicates obstinacy. With curved, smooth contours it indicates both obstinacy and idleness.

When a head in profile is wider than it is long, with straight edged contours, this indicates inflexibility and wickedness. With curved, smooth contours it indicates sensuality, looseness, idleness and voluptuousness.

Line 58   The Bible states that God 'created heaven and earth', and placed a 'firmanent in the midst of the waters', i.e. that God produced matter where there had been none before – everything was newly formed and did not evolve or change. Not everyone held this opinion.

Ane Prayer for the Pest

Ane Prayer for the Pest

O eterne God! of power infinyt,
To quhois hie knawlege na thing is obscure
That is, or was, or evir sal be, perfyt,
Into Thy sicht, quhill that this warld indure;
Haif mercy of us, indigent and peure;
Thow dois na wrang to puneis our offens:
O Lord, that is to mankynd haill succure,
Preserve us fra this perrelus pestilens.

We The beseik, O Lord of Lordis all,
Thy eiris inclyne and heir our grit regrait;   10
We ask remeid of The in general,
That is of help and confort desolait;
Bot Thow with rewth our hairtis recreate,
We ar bot deid but only Thy clemens:
We The exhort on kneis law prostrait,
Preserve us from this perrellus pestilens!

We ar richt glaid Thow puneis our trespass
Be ony kind of uthir tribulatioun,
Wer it Thy will, O Lord of Hevin, allaiss,
That we suld thus be haistily put doun   20
And de as beistis, without confessioun,
That nane dar mak with uthir residence.
O Blissit Jesu, that woir the thorny croun,
Preserve us from this perrelus pestilens!

Use derth, O Lord, or seiknes, and hungir soir,
And slak Thy plaig that is so penetryve.
The pepill ar perreist: quha may remeid thairfoir,
Bot Thow, O Lord, that for thame lost Thy lyve?
Suppois our syn be to The pungityve,
Our deid ma nathing our synnys recompens.   30
Haif mercy, Lord! we ma nocht with The stryve.
Preserve us from this perrellus pestilens.

Haif mercy, Lord! haif mercy, Hevynis King!
Haif mercy of Thy pepill penetent;
Haif mercy of our petous punissing;
Retreit the sentence and Thy just jugement
Aganis us synnaris, that servis to be schent
Without mercy; we ma mak no defens.
Thow that, but rewth, upoun the Rude was rent,
Preserve us from this perrellus pestilens.   40

A Prayer for the Pest

O eternal God of power infinite,
In whose great knowledge there is no obscurity.
About the fact that nothing is, was, or ever shall be, perfect,
In Your sight, as long as this world will endure;
Have mercy on us, indigent and poor;
You do no wrong to punish our offence;
O Lord, who is to mankind whole succor,
Preserve us from this perilous pestilence.

We beseech you, O Lord of Lords all,
Your ears incline and hear our great regret;   10
We ask redress of You in general,
We who are of help and comfort desolate.
Unless You with pity our hearts alleviate,
We are but dead without Your lenience.
We exhort You, on knees low, prostrate,
Preserve us from this perilous pestilence.

Glad would we be if You punished our trespass
By any other kind of tribulation.
If it were Your will, O Lord of heaven, alas,
That we should thus be hastily put down,   20
And die as beasts, without confession,
That none dare with another make residence.
O Blessed Jesus, that wore the thorny crown,
Preserve us from this perilous pestilence.

Use dearth, O Lord, or sickness, and hunger sore,
And slake Your plague that is so penetrative.
Your people have perished: who may amend therefore,
But You, O Lord, who for them ceased to live?
Suppose our sin be to You afflictive,
Our death may not our sins recompense.   30
Have mercy, Lord, we may not with Thee strive.
Preserve us from this perilous pestilence.

Have mercy, Lord. Have mercy, Heaven's King!
Have mercy on Your people penitent;
Have mercy with our piteous punishing;
Retract the sentence of Your just judgment
Against us sinners who deserve punishment
Without mercy; we may make no defence.
You, who without pity, on the cross were rent,
Preserve us from this perilous pestilence.   40
Remember, Lord, how dear You have us bought,

Remember, Lord! how deir Thow hes us bocht,
That for us synnaris sched Thy pretius blude,
Now to redeme that Thow hes maid of nocht,
That is of vertew barrane and denude;
Haif rewth, Lord, of Thyn Awin symilitude;
Puneis with pety and nocht with violens.
We knaw it is for our ingratitude
That we ar puneist with this pestilens.

Thow grant us grace for till amend our miss,
And till evaid this crewall suddane deid   50
We knaw our sin is all the cause of this,
For oppin syn thair is set no remeid.
The justice of God mon puneis than bot dreid,
For by the law He will with non dispens:
Quhair justice laikis, thair is eternall feid,
Of God that suld preserf fra pestilens.

Bot wald the heiddismen, that suld keip the law
Puneiss the peple for thair transgressioun,
Thair wald na deid the peple than ourthaw:
Bot thay ar gevin sa planely till oppressioun,   60
That God will nocht heir thair intercessioun;
Bot all ar punist for inobediens
Be sword or deid withouttin remissioun,
And hes just caus to send us pestilens.

Superne Lucerne! guberne this pestilens,
Preserve and serve that we not sterve thairin.
Declyne that pyne, be Thy devyne prudens.
For Trewth, haif rewth lat not our slewth us twin:
Oursyt, full tyt, wer we contryt, wald blin.
Dissiver did never, quha evir The besocht: 70
Send grace, with space, and us imbrace fra syn.
Latt nocht be tynt that Thow so deir hes bocht.

O Prince preclair, this cair cotidiane,
We The exhort, distort it in exyle;
Bot Thow remeid, this deid is bot ane trane
For to dissaif the laif, and thame begyle.
Bot Thow, sa wyis, devyis to mend this byle
Of this mischief, quha ma releif us ocht?
For wrangus win, bot Thow our syn oursyll:
Lat nocht be tynt that Thow so deir hes bocht   80

That for us sinners shed Your precious blood,
Now to redeem that which You made of naught,
That is of virtue barren and denude,
Have pity, Lord, of Your Own similitude;
Punish with pity and not with violence.
We know it is for our ingratitude
That we are punished with this pestilence.

Grant us grace to amend our misdeeds
To evade dying, cruelly, suddenly;   50
We know our sins are all the cause of this,
For blatant sin there is no set remedy.
The justice of God must punish undoubtedly,
For by the law He will with none dispense;
When Justice fails there remains the eternal enmity
Of God, that should protect from pestilence.

Unless those leaders, who should uphold the law
Punish the people for their transgression,
No death would the people then overthrow;
But they are given so clearly to oppression,   60
That God will not hear their intercession;
So all are punished for their disobedience
By sword or death without remission.
And He has just cause to send us pestilence.

Supreme Light, control this pestilence,
Preserve and grant that we are not starving.
Reduce that pain by Your divine prudence.
For truth, have mercy. Let not our sloth mean parting.
Were we contrite our sorrow would quickly be ceasing.
Cast away never, whoever You besought,   70
Send grace, with time, and set us free from sinning.
Let naught be lost that You so dear have bought,

O renowned prince, this sorrow daily,
We You exhort to turn it aside in exile.
Unless You redress this deed it is but trickery,
To deceive the rest and them beguile.
Unless You, so wise, seek to mend this boil
Of this downfall, who may relieve us aught
Of wrongful gain, unless You our sin conceal.
Let naught be lost that You so dear have bought.   80

Now for our vice, which justice must correct,

Sen for our vyce that justice mon correct,
O King Most Hie, now pacifie Thy feid:
Our syn is huge, refuge we not suspect;
As Thou art Juge, deluge us of this dreid.
In tyme assent, or we be schent with deid;
We us repent all tyme mispent forthocht:
Thairfoir, evirmoir be gloir to Thy Godheid
Lat nocht be tynt that Thow sa deir hes bocht.

Notes

The Pest   Three types of the plague have been recorded, the bubonic, the pneumonic, and
the septicemic. The second variation, the pneumonic, appears to be the type
experienced in Dunfermline in 1439 when those affected died within two days
of the onset of the disease. There was also a famine in Scotland in that year and
the people believed that the wrath of God, exhibited by the famine and by the
pest, had descended upon them in order to make them mend their ways.

In 1499 the plague again raged in Dunfermline having reached there from
Edinburgh. It was known as the 'grandgore.' It appears that the poem 'The
Prayer for the Pest' may have been written before the onset of the disease and
is a plea to God not to punish those in Dunfermline by allowing it to spread to
the town. There is a tradition that Henryson died of plague.

Lines 65-88   The final three stanzas employ internal rhyme, which somewhat disturbs the
sense in order to produce three rhymes in each line of the antepenultimate
and two rhymes in the last two stanzas. This kind of virtuoso performance
was quite common in Middle Scots and Middle English poems, and seeks to
bring the poem to a particularly forceful conclusion. It has not been possible to
replicate this within the translation.

O King Most High, now pacify Your enmity;
Our sin is great, a repeal we do not expect;
As You are judge remove from us this anxiety.
In time assent or we be undone in entirety,
We do repent. The misspent time our thought;
Therefore evermore be glory to Your Divinity
Let naught be lost that You so dear have bought.

The Want of Wyse Men

The Want of Wyse Men

Me ferlyis of this grete confusioun,
I wald sum clerk of connyng walde declerde,
Quhat gerris this warld be turnyt upside doun.
Thair is na faithfull fastness founde in erd;
Now is nocht thre may traistly trow the ferde;
Welth is away, and wit is worthin wynkis;
Now sele is sorow, this is a wofull werde,
Sen want of wyse men makis fulis to sit on binkis.

As bukis beiris witnes, quhen levit King Saturnus,
For gudely governance this warld was goldin cald;   10
For untreuth we wate nocht quhare-to it turnis;
The quhill that Octaviane, the monarchy could hald,
Our-all was pes, well set as hertis wald,
Than regnyt reule, and resone held his rynkis;
Now lakkis prudence: nobilitee is thralde,
Sen want of wyse men makis fulis to sit on bynkis.

Aristotill for his moralitee,
Austyn, or Ambrose, for dyvine scripture,
Quha can placebo, and nocht half dirige,
That practik for to pike and pill the pure,   20
He sall cum in, and thay stand at the dure;
For wardly wyn sik walkis, quhen wysar wynkis;
Wit takis na worschip, sik is the aventure,
Sen want of wyse men makis fulis to sit on binkis.

Now, but defense, rycht lyis all desolate,
Rycht na resone under na rufe has rest;
Youth is but raddour, and age is obstynate,
Mycht but mercy; the pure ar all opprest.
Lerit folk suld tech the peple of the best;
Thouch lare be lytil, yit ferles in tham sinkis: 30
It may noucht be this warld ay thus suld lest,
That want of wyse men makis fulis sit on binkis.

For now is exilde all ald noble corage,
Lautee, lufe, and liberalitee;
Now is stabilitee fundin in na stage,
Nor degest counsele wyth maturitee;
Peas is away, all in perplexitee;
Prudence and policy ar banyst our al brinkis:
This warld is wer, sa may it callit be,
That want of wyse men makis fulis sit on bynkis.   40

The Want of Wise Men

I marvel at this great confusion.
I wish some clerk of learning would state freely,
What causes this world to be turned in such distortion.
On earth there is not found faithful constancy;
There are not three who may believe the fourth safely;
Prosperity has gone, and all wit has become guile;
Now happiness is sorrow. This is a woeful destiny,
Since want of wise men causes fools to sit in courts.

As books bear witness, when lived the king Saturn,
For good government this world was golden called;   10
For untruth we know not where-to it may turn;
The time that Octavian, the monarch reigned,
Over all was peace, just as all hearts wanted,
Then order ruled and reason held its ranks;
Now prudence is lacking, nobility enslaved,
Since want of wise men causes fools to sit in courts.

Aristotle for his moral belief,
Augustine, or Ambrose, for divine scripture,
Whoever can flatter, and not suffer grief,
That practice to steal and dupe the poor,   20
He shall prosper, while they stand at the door;
For the worldly keep alert while wise men close their eyes;
Wit is not worshipped. Such is the outcome,
Since want of wise men causes fools to sit in courts.

Now, without defence, right lies all desolate,
Neither right nor reason under any roof has rest;
Youth has but terror, and age is obstinate,
Might without mercy, the poor are all oppressed,
Learned folk should teach the people of the best,
Though learning is little, wonders are absorbed.   30
It may not be this world, always thus, should last,
That want of wise men cause fools to sit in courts.

For now is exiled all old noble bravery,
Loyalty, love and liberality;
Now in no stage is found stability,
Nor considered counsel with maturity;
Peace has gone, all in perplexity;
Prudence and policy are banished over all sides.
This world is failing so may it reasoned be,
That want of wise men causes fools to sit in courts   40

Quhare is the balance of just and equitie?
Nothir meryt is preisit, na punyst is trespas;
All ledis lyvis lawles at libertee,
Noucht reulit be reson, mare than ox or ass;
Gude faith is flemyt worthin fraellar than glas;
Trew lufe is lorne, and lautee haldis no lynkis;
Sik governance I call noucht worth a fasse,
Sen want of wise men makis fulis sitt on binkis.

Now wrang hes warrane, and law is bot wilfulness;
Quha hes the war is worthin on him all the wyte   50
For trewth is tressoun, and faith is fals fekilness;
Gyle is now gyd, and vane lust is also delyte;
Kirk is contempnit, thay compt nocht cursing a myte;
Grit God is grevit, that we rycht soir forthinkis:
The causs of this ony man may sone vit,
That want of wys men garis fulis sit on binkis.

Luve hes tane leif, and wirschep hes no udir wane;
With passing poverty pryd is importable;
Vyce is bot vertew, wit is with will soir ourgane;
As lairdis so laddis, daly chengeable;   60
But ryme or ressone all is bot heble-hable;
Sic sturtfull stering in to Godis neise it stinkis;
Both He haif rew, all is unremedable,
For want of wyse men makis fulis sit on binkis.

O Lord of Lordis! God and Gouvernour,
Makar and Movar, bath of mare and lesse,
Quhais power, wisedome, and he honoure,
Is infynite, sal be, and evir wes,
As in the principall mencioun of the Messe,
All thir sayd thingis reforme as Thou best thinkis;   70
Quhilk ar degradit, for pure pitee redresse,
Sen want of wise men makis fulis sit in binkis

Where is the balance of justice and equity?
Neither merit is praised, no trespass punished alas.
All people live lawless at liberty,
Nothing ruled by reason, more than ox or ass.
Good faith is banished, become frailer than glass;
True love is lost and loyalty holds no ties.
Such governing I think not worth a blade of grass,
Since want of wise men makes fools to sit in courts.

Now wrong has authority and law is but wilfulness.
Who suffers most on him the blame alights,   50
For truth is treason and faith is false fickleness.
Guile is now good and vain lust is also delight.
The church is despised, they hold not cursing a mite.
Great God is grieving, that fills me with regrets:
The cause of this any man may soon know it right,
That want of wise men causes fools to sit in courts.

Love has taken leave and worship has no finite purpose;
With passing poverty, pride is unbearable;
Vice is but virtue, reason overcome with lustfulness.
Lairds and servants, constantly changeable;   60
Without rhyme or reason all is but hubble bubble.
Such contentious action in God's nose it stinks.
Unless He has pity all is unredeemable,
For want of wise men causes fools to sit in courts.

O Lord of Lords, God and Governor,
Maker and Mover, both of more and less.
Whose power, wisdom, and high honour
Is infinite, shall be and ever was,
As in the principle statement of the mass,
Reform as You think all these said things;   70
Whoever is degraded, for pure pity redress,
Since want of wise men causes fools to sit in courts.

Notes

This poem may be found in the text by Chepman and Myllar, printed without title or author's name. It follows on from Orpheus and Eurydice as another ballad and has been accepted by inference as Henryson's.

Line 8	'Want of wyse men makis fulis to sit on binkis.' was a common proverb and may be found in 'Scottish Proverbs', Andrew Henderson, 1876 and in 'The Carmichaell Collection', 1957, these publications containing some proverbs from the fifteen century.
	Binks – benches or high stations in life.
	'causes fools to sit on binks' – causes fools to sit on the bench in law courts, in high places at the royal court or in positions of authority. The law courts were being run badly at this time with the proper procedures not being followed and the king was taking advice from men who had no real position or influence in the land but who sat in high places in his court. Either situation could be being referred to here.
Lines 9-12	Presumably a reference 1) to the legendary Golden Age when men lived in harmony and prosperity together and 2) to the historical Age of Augustus (Octavian) in Rome where the Roman Empire guaranteed peace and prosperity.
Line 17	Aristotle (384 BCE): Greek ethical, metaphysical and political philosopher.
Line 18	Augustine of Hippo (354-430): Latin Father and Doctor of the Church. His *Confessions* (c400) and *The City of God* (after 412) are testaments of Christian piety and belief.
	Ambrose (c 340-397): Bishop of Milan and leader of the early Christian Church.

Bibliography

Carmichaell, James (d.1628): *Proverbs in Scots,* Edinburgh University Press, 1957.

Comrie, J.D.: *The History of Medicine to 1860.* Balliere, Tindall & Cox, 1927.

Hamilton, David: *The Healers. The History of Medicine in Scotland,* Cannongate, 1981.

Lewis, C.S.: *The Allegory of Love,* Oxford University Press, 1958.

Macfarlane, Leslie J.: *William Elphinstone and the Kingdom of Scotland 1431-1514,* Aberdeen University Press, 1985.

Metcalf, W.M.: *The Poems of Robert Henryson,* Alexander Gardener, 1917.

Poulton, E.P.:*Taylor's Practice of Medicine, 15th edition,* J & A Churchill Ltd, London, 1936.

Simpson, W.D.: *Quartercentenery of the Death of Henry Boece in 1536,* Aberdeen University Press, 1937.

Smith, Gregory: *The Days of James IV,* David Nutt, 1900.

Smith, Gregory: *Specimens of Middle Scots,* William Blackwood & Sons, Edinburgh & London, 1902.

Stevenson, George: *Pieces from the Makculloch and Gray Mss.* William Blackwood & Sons, Edinburgh & London, 1918.

The Holy Bible, Odham's Press Ltd, 1949.

Dictionaries

Compact Oxford English Dictionary, Clarendon Press, 1994.

Craigie, Sir William A.: *A Dictionary from the Older Scottish Tongue from 12th to the end of the 17th century* – Vols. 1-10, University of Chicago, Chicago & London.

Funk, Charles Earle: *New Practical Standard Dictionary,* Funk & Wagnall Co. 1946.

Grant, W. Editor: *The Scottish National Dictionary,* (All the Scottish words to be in use or to have been in use since c. 1700), vols 1-10, Neill & Co. Ltd. Edinburgh, 1941.

Johnson, Samuel: *A Dictionary of the English Language,* Joseph Ogle Robinson, London, 1828.

Salmon, William: *The Family Dictionary or Household Companion,* Printed for A. Rhodes at the Star, the corner of Bride-lane in Fleet Street in London, (1696?)